# Ex&Drugs

# Ex&Drugs

*a memoir*

## JESSICA KOZNER

**FCP**

*Full Court Press*
*Englewood Cliffs, New Jersey*

*First Edition*

Copyright © 2024 by Jessica Kozner

Published in the United States of America
by Full Court Press, 601 Palisade Avenue,
Englewood Cliffs, NJ 07632
*fullcourtpress.com*

ISBN 978-1-953728-23-4
Library of Congress Control No. 2024900046

*Editing and book design by Barry Sheinkopf*

TO MY HUSBAND

*who accepts me as I am and as I was*

TO MY CHILDREN

*who I hope never read this*

AND TO MY MOTHER

*I'm so sorry, and also, you were right*

# LOSING IT

MY BOYFRIEND, BEN, IS COMING OVER to break up with me. Well, I'm not *sure* that's what he's coming to do, but we're going to have a "talk" about the magic that's gone, and it didn't sound too promising when we spoke on the phone a little while ago. He's allergic to my cats, so he rarely visits. I'm joking to myself that at least now he *has* to come over. It wouldn't be right for him to have me cab over there just to tell me, in so many words, to leave—for good.

How do I feel? Upset. But it's *my* upset, the Oh-it's-so-tragic-what-a-good-story-I'll-have-for-my-friends or the This-is-just-what-I-need-to-get-back-into-the-swing-of-things-at-work kind. I want to let myself mourn, but until we talk, I can't really consider this a loss since I'm not sure what we will say. If we do break up, I imagine I will still have difficulty grieving. I'll cry some real tears, then force some more, then I'll look in the mirror and stare at what a beautiful light green my eyes become when I cry. It's true. I don't generally buy this my-eyes-change-color stuff. I think people's eyes just look different in different light or when they wear different colors. But my hazel eyes really do turn a kind of pale aqua when I've been crying—in *any* light.

And see, here I am thinking about anything but the subject at hand. This man, boy practically, is no longer smitten, and he says it's as painful for him as it is for me. He wants to be psyched to see me when I come over. But he's not.

THIS NEW DEVELOPMENT IS QUITE RECENT, perhaps it's been for the last week or so, but we've only been dating for about a month and a half, so everything is quite recent. We've known each other for five months. We've dated since we met at a bar downtown but not *exclusively* until last month or so.

I don't know what to do. What's worse, I don't know how to feel. On the one hand, I think that Ben could really be the love of my life, or at least the love of my adult life. Then I think, Maybe he's not, and I just think he is. But then I think, Doesn't thinking it's the case make it so? I mean, how can love be measured except by thoughts and feelings? Then I think, Well, even if this *is* the love of my life that doesn't mean:

1. There can't be another.
2. We should necessarily be together in spite of our love for one another.

I'm not sure two people definitely belong together even if they are the loves of each other's lives. I decided some time ago that love is not the glue that holds relationships together. Frankly, I am not sure what is, but I think lots of people who love each other can't make it work regardless of the depths of their emotions.

I hope this is the case—I mean, *not* the case—with us. I hope we can stay together in spite of my Freudian typo. I hope we stay together, but I fear we won't. Will my doubt and insecurity jinx it? Might I really *want* to break up? If so, is that just a defense mechanism, like I say that I want to break up because I feel I can't prevent the inevitable? But why should it be inevitable? Do I have any power over this other person? Should I exercise it if I do?

BEN JUST CALLED. I BEGAN WRITING AS SOON as I got home, while I was waiting for him to call to say he's coming over. He's coming over! I'm scared but excited in that sociopathically removed way that I get when things are heavy, like I, too, am anxious to see the plot unfold. I am as eager as you are, whoever you are. I may be a bit more eager. However, I feel a dread you surely don't, so perhaps you are more eager, since it's not your relationship on the line. Or at least not yours with Ben. . . as far as I know. You may have your own relationship troubles. Probably you do. A comforting thought. I like the idea of you miserable at the moment. Not more than I am, just equally. But if you're happy, more power to you. Why should everything be such a big fucking deal? Why is it so hard to be happy, and why is it so devastating when we're not? Why do we even expect to be happy? Or do we not expect but just want happiness because it feels good? Is that a normal state of being? I ask this sincerely and not rhetorically. Are we supposed to be happy, or is it just nicer that way?

He's going to be here any minute! My stomach is messed up—not hurting, just weird. Obviously, it's nerves. I hate caring. I'll try to let you know what happens, but I warn you now there's a chance you won't hear from me for a while—or maybe ever again—if things go well, because I am most productive when conflicted, and much less creative when at peace.

He's not here yet, and I can't do anything but write. I can't just sit. I can't listen to music. I can't watch TV— well, unless *Absolutely Fabulous* is on, and it will be, I just realized, in half an hour, and I'll have to miss it so that Ben can have my undivided attention while he breaks up with me. I'm feeling a bit victimized at the moment. I am comfortable in that role. It takes a lot of the pressure off. I once had a boyfriend—we were living together (and talk about the magic being gone, and there was barely even any magic to begin with)—but I couldn't bring myself to break up with him. I had to make him do it, and then it was fine and I felt free, but if I had broken up with him, I wouldn't have stopped questioning whether or not it was the right thing to do. I probably would have convinced myself that I'd been madly in love with him, which I wasn't, and that he was wonderfully interesting and absolutely perfect for me, which he wasn't.

ALRIGHT, WELL, THAT'S SETTLED. BEN'S COME AND GONE and all in time for me to catch *AbFab*. Our talk only lasted about twenty minutes. He tried suggesting we see other people, but I couldn't. Maybe I should have. No, too terrible. I can't. Would it have worked? I don't think so. So I suggested that we just end things.

Did I really think that or did I just want to be the one to say it, or to not be the one to hear it? Anyway, he seemed to like the idea very much. Gave me some bull about wishing he could say everything would be OK but he couldn't. He thanked me for being so rational. I didn't cry. I could have but chose not to. I'm writing this during the commercial. The most painful thing he said was that he's come to see me more as a friend than as a lover or girlfriend. I knew that this was horrible, the way he meant it, but I tried to put a positive spin on it and remind him of the flip-side, that we're like *best* friends and that

that's what made the relationship so enjoyable. But he thought the romance had somehow gone and we were *just* friends.

Then there was some time when we didn't speak and just sat there. I thought about trying to talk him out of it but decided against that. Then he said something awful, especially so because I think he meant it to be comforting. He asked, cheerfully, if I, too, could imagine us, in years to come, as friends, in love with other people and joking about the fact that we had once dated. This was of no help.

And now I am crying. I think it's good. Would rather not be feeling so bad, though. I'm noticing my sentences have become a bit Joycean—not that they are genius, but that I have that stream-of-consciousness thing going.

Whom to call? Will Mom say, "I told you so?" I know she'll think it. That's OK, but will she *say* it? Kim's in Bayside, celebrating her dead mother's birthday. Can't call her. Abigail? Too out of touch, won't relate. Maybe that's a good thing. She'll make light of this tragedy. She's become somewhat embittered since middle school. She'll ask, "What did you expect of a child who's never had a girlfriend before?" And she'll be right. I could call her. But what if she's out? Getting her answering machine at a time like this would feel worse than not calling at all. Wish I were crazy enough to call my shrink right now, but I'm not. This is not *that kind* of emergency. Or maybe I'm just not that kind of person, fortunately.

Called Abigail, no answer. At least there was no machine. No teary message for me to leave. Called my old
boyfriend, David. He's the one I lived with. Rationality
personified. M.D., Ph.D. Both from Ivies. Brilliant. All
science, though. His genius was of little use in our relationship, but it could be handy at a time like this.

Actually, it was, somewhat. He talked about how
much emphasis I place upon being in a relationship and
how much my self-worth hinges upon whether I'm dating
someone. It stung to hear that I view myself as a little
more than a reflection of my mate, but there is truth to
it. He pointed out that I can learn to do things just for me
and be just as happy and productive without a partner.
When I think about it, there's a chance that I am, in fact,
*only* productive without a partner, but that's a discussion
for another time. I agree that I would be a much happier
person if I were comfortable being alone, but it's going to
be a long road. Actually, if I'm being honest, I probably
am only comfortable alone but only if I can say I am in a
relationship. I suppose this has more than a little to do
with my parents and my upbringing, but at twenty-seven,
even *I* have grown weary of blaming my parents. They did
their best, and it's all fairly moot at this point.

Anyhow, I got off the phone with David and feeling
mildly saner though vaguely weirded out that I've just wept
to an old beau about this break-up with Ben. I mean, David
and I are just friends, but he *is* my most recent long-term

boyfriend, and I think I propelled us abruptly into a new phase of friendship by calling him up sobbing. While we chat occasionally, we had not previously shared really intimate thoughts and feelings about other relationships. We'd not even really shared intimate thoughts and feelings about our own relationship. Mostly he liked to hear about my sexual fantasies involving other women while we were fucking. He was helpful in his dry, doctor way and, though I have no desire to be back together with him, I would have liked just a bit less objectivity and detached neighborliness and maybe a pinch of jealousy as I blubbered on about Ben. But that's just because I'm insecure. I know I'm much better off having David behave as he did, as much as I would have enjoyed a little ego-stroking. (Actually, secure or not, who doesn't like having their ego stroked?)

Coincidentally, John, a guy I stopped dating to go out with Ben, called while I was on the phone with dry Dr. David. I ended things with John whenever it was that Ben and I made our steadydom official. I had been dating John casually for a short time before meeting Ben. Fuckin' Ben just swept me off my feet, and apparently I had had that same effect on John, who was heartbroken when we split. I was actually sort of sorry to see him go but I preferred the prospect of monogamy with Ben to any of my other options, which included that same scenario with John.

When I returned John's call, I told him that Ben and I had broken up. I told him partly because he could tell by my voice that I had been crying and partly because David's speech about me not needing a boyfriend fell on not quite deaf, but somewhat hearing-impaired, ears. Basically, I think David is right but I can't imagine living the way he does, preoccupied with his job and his inventions and patents and proud and gratified at the end of each productive day. A day is productive for me if:

1. I buy some clothing or makeup I especially like.
2. I don't eat something outrageously fattening or, better still, I don't eat.
3. I have a boyfriend.

The above items are actually listed in reverse order of importance.

Telling John I broke up with Ben was mostly my way of feeling him out, seeing if he's still interested. I knew beforehand that he was, but you know me and my pea-sized ego, trying endlessly to make at least a lima bean of it.

A few concerns about the plans I made to see John tomorrow after getting off the phone with David:

1. Am I doing it solely as a rebound maneuver?
2. Will I break his heart again? I don't want to hurt him. I really can't stand the thought of fucking him over a second time. He's a gentle, lovely soul . . . And he's a lawyer!

3. Will the sex be as bad this go-round as it was when we were last together?

4. How much, or little, do I care about the fact that he's not Jewish, or the fact that I am (though not practicing)?

5. Should I try being on my own for a while?

Already I can answer question #5. No. I'm not up for that. Don't want it. Tried, admittedly not for very long, but for a few months, to do the alone thing, and I recall feeling very alone. I don't care if this is a problem; it's not one I feel ready to tackle right now. Admittedly, "right now" might turn into "this lifetime," but we'll cross that bridge when we come to it. The question is not whether or not I should rush into a new relationship. That is completely my intention. The question is: Should I rush into it with *John?* I suspect I should not. I fear I am not in love with him. I fear I may find my own insanity and/or neediness, and his love for me, sufficient grounds to date and who-knows-what-else this very sweet guy who I should probably leave alone. I guess I'm jumping ahead a bit.

By the way, I can't believe Ben hasn't called. I'm as worried that he will as that he won't. I more worry he won't. Not that I would necessarily get back together with him if he did, just, how can he not call? It's *me* he's not calling. How can he not call *me?* Yes, I'm being completely narcissistic, but I am also me. Me, me, me. You know, *me*. I am the only me, and these other girls aren't. Why must he abandon me for them? Of course, what's really the case is that he left me, not for them, but for himself, which is different and in some ways more, and in others, less painful.

*Is* Ben going to call? If so, when? What will be my response if and when he does? And why, as I approach thirty, do I still have to sound and act like a fucking Judy Blume character? And not one of those steamy, grown-up Judy Blume book characters, but the kids'-book kind of character. You know the ones. They're concerned about braces and zits and boys. I think one had a back problem. One was really fat. Another lost her virginity under yucky circumstances.

It's getting late, and I'm tired and spent, and as I write this I'm beginning to care too much about things like grammar and punctuation. That means I've calmed down, which is good since I feel better, but bad because I don't want my writing to be self-conscious or contrived. I want to tell my truth and not try to impress you, which is what I fear I may be headed for if I keep writing. So I'm going to stop for now. Hopefully, I'll stay sad enough to continue expressing myself freely, because I think it's really therapeutic and cathartic, and to quote one of my all-time favorite movies, *Spinal Tap*, "It makes a swell gift, too!"

# MORNING #1

AM UP AND MISERABLE AND OUT OF CIGARETTES. I think I've figured out why Ben broke up with me. I'm not sure I know the exact reason, but it might have at least something to do with it. I stumbled upon my hypothesis last night. It makes the entire break-up seem so silly and needless and really my fault almost entirely. And more importantly, I think the process of writing it down will be so painful that some good will have to come from confronting it. I mean, I am so acutely averse to confronting this idea I intend to share that I know I will somehow benefit from doing so. I don't know, though, if I can do it without cigarettes and coffee. I'm going to the store. I'll be back in a little while with the heartbreaking and absurd story of the real reason why Ben and I broke up. It's so crazy.

Two quick things before I go. Did I mention that one of my concerns regarding John is that he's gay? I don't really worry that he is a practicing, HIV-exposure-risking, underground-club-going gay guy. In fact, I don't think *he* thinks he's gay. And of course, maybe he's not, but isn't every effeminate man actually gay? I feel they are. To me, there are two types of gay guys, those who seem gay and those who don't; on the other hand, there is only one type of straight guy, the type who seems straight. I could be wrong, but it is a concern I have regarding John. My friend Amy always talks about guys who have twinkly eyes seeming gay. She says not all guys who seem gay actually are. But I don't know if I agree. I don't remember the other thing I had to say.

I'M BACK. GOT TWO PACKS OF CIGARETTES. I never do that. I'm really psyched to have extras. Two funny thoughts I had as I fought back the tears on my cigarette run, but first here's a different thought, one I just had: It seems my thoughts are the only things in my life that come in pairs. Get it? A silly break-up joke. Anyway, first I thought, What if the doorman sees me crying in spite of the fact that I am wearing big, dark glasses? He has worked in the building for ages, and I've lived here on and off since I was a little kid, for twenty-two years now. He must've seen all kinds of shit go on here—deaths, divorces, etc. I'm sure he's seen other tenants cry. We're kind of pals. I like him.

He's very funny, always ragging on our inappropriate and obnoxious superintendent, Charlie. At some point maybe I'll tell you some funny Charlie stories. So I thought there was a chance that if he saw me crying, he might ask me what was wrong, and it struck me as funny that I could say, "Oh, I just heard some super-sad news—about myself." It's not funny now that I've expressed it, but I liked it in the elevator. Maybe you see the humor in it. Actually, it stems from a joke I had in college with my roommate, Gwen. Somehow, I started referring to stories about stuff, especially painful or embarrassing stuff that happened to me, as "gossip." Maybe it helped me distance myself from the sting and shame of what had happened. Like I would say, "Gwen, I've got some really good gossip about me." I don't know what it means. It's probably more of that sociopathically removed shit.

The other funny thought I had was that I am working on a proposal for a course I'd like to teach at The Learning Annex. It's some bullshit about how to lead a happier life. I was chock full of ideas when my life was happier. There's been some discussion among my friends about whether it would be better for me to mail or hand-deliver this proposal. I already called the guy at the place, and he made it perfectly clear that he wants me just to send it in and not stop by. But I'm attractive and could make a good impression, one that might sway him, because, you know, it's true for the most part that better-looking people sometimes get stuff ugly ones don't. Anyway, as I rode down the elevator in my filthy flannel shirt, baggy jeans that had belonged to Ben, beat-up clogs, dark glasses, no makeup, no bra, tits flapping limply about, and tear streaks running down my cheeks, I thought, How funny would it be if I bumped into The Learning Annex guy, the one to whom I want to pitch my outline on how to be a happier, more together person.

I just spoke to Kim, who was very helpful and supportive last night. We spoke for a while after I stopped writing. She can be super-comforting, and I don't feel embarrassed crying to her. I read some of last night's entry to her and she liked it. I read some of this morning's entry to her, and she liked it less. She couldn't say precisely why. She's coming over soon. I feel like I've lost some momentum, but I'm not done trying to get these thoughts down.

Ben just called, and we talked for a little while. I'll have to tell you about it later, since Kim just got here. Before I go, Kim told me that she thinks the part of the story she doesn't like is that I keep calling it a "story" when it is, as she put it, "a dramatic monologue in the tradition of Robert Browning," and also that I keep addressing you, the reader. She thinks that is stylized and contrived. I asked her how she could think that, since she knows that this writing is wholly unplanned and from the bottom of my heart. She seemed to think that was a sweet sentiment. She just made a point of telling me she doesn't think my talking to you, the reader, is so much bad as it is not in keeping with the rest of my "story." She's telling me to write that I have to go because she just poured the coffee, which she also graciously made upon arriving.

She also just said, "Fuck Ben. Can I call him?" I don't think either of us really wants that to happen. She's watching me write this. "Actually, I think I *would* like to call him," she adds. I don't want her to (Kim, please don't), and now we are going to have coffee.

KIM JUST LEFT. SHE ONLY STAYED A COUPLE of hours because, at 3:00 p.m., she had to pick up the kids she baby-sits. They're seven and ten years old. She's worked for them for six years or so. Actually, I should say that she's worked for their parents for that long, but these kids, because of their parents, are all too aware of the fact that Kim is an employee. They're nice kids, they just know too much for their ages, especially, Jennifer, the older one. When she was four, Jennifer asked Kim for a cookie, got one, asked for another, got it, and upon being refused a third cookie announced, "If you don't give me that cookie right now, I'll tell Mommy, and she'll fire you." Apparently they're less bratty now.

Anyway, back to Ben. He called before Kim arrived, but I was on the phone with my friend Liz from work. I was in the process of telling Liz about the break-up when the call-waiting went off. I was deliberately abrupt with him and told him it wasn't a good time for me to talk and essentially hung up on him as he was starting to say something. Then I went back to my call with Liz. I told her that it'd been Ben who called, and I asked did she think I should call him back. She said that I should at least find out why he called, and we agreed that it was uncool of me to just cut him off like that. I was being childish. And rude.

I called back a few minutes later. He asked me how I'm doing, and the concern in his voice really annoyed me. Like *he's* fine and just wants to make sure that *I* am not suicidal. Fuck that. So I told him I'm OK, which in fact I am, although I wouldn't be surprised if I have another hellish surge of longing and remorse at some point soon.

He had called to tell me that he got some job in real estate which is easy enough to do if you can walk and speak some English. I know because I am in real estate. Maybe it takes more than that to do well, but getting the job is a breeze. There's so much turnover in the business and they don't pay you, it's all commission, so brokers really don't have much to lose if you suck. I guess you're using their desk space and phone and fax, etc. But it's not the same as when they've got to give you a salary and benefits and stuff. So I congratulated him and asked him if he had any additional insights today now that some time has passed.

He told me that he didn't think anything he might say would be productive. I braced myself and asked him what that meant. "Well, I know I love you," he said. He was right. It wasn't much help because, then, why are we apart? But I admit that it was a better insight than, "You know, last night was the best night of my life! Our break-up. . .healthiest thing I could've done!" Then he asked if I wanted to remain friends, and I said I wasn't sure. Not, I don't think, to hurt him, but because I am genuinely not sure. I think he might've suggested the seeing-each-other-and-other-people thing again, but I might be making that up. If he did, once again I declined.

Then I read him some of this "dramatic monologue," or whatever this is, and I'm not sure I should have. I don't think it hurt or helped us in terms of any kind of recon-ciliation; I just don't think I should open myself up to him, and be vulnerable, right now. Also, I'm sure it must have stroked his ego, and that's the last thing I want to do.

I don't want to see John tonight. I was stupid to make plans with him. Did I do it because I don't want to be alone? To get back at Ben even if he isn't jealous at all? Maybe it was just one of those silly impulsive acts, but are those ever just that? Can any act be meaningless?

Well, whatever it was, I don't want to see him tonight. Question is, do I not want to see him at all, or do I not want to see him so soon after a painful break-up? I think part of why I agreed to see him—because I know he loves me and felt like that would be comforting—is the very reason I'm having second thoughts. I don't want to see someone who loves me while someone I love does not.

Anyway, I'm not going to cancel. He's probably in his bar review class now anyway, but that's not why. Is it mean to cancel? No, it's probably meaner to see him. Then why not cancel? He asked me when I left him for Ben if a marriage proposal would change my mind. God, if only Ben liked me that much. What if I had said, "Yes"? What if he had replied, "Oh, just asking." That would've been funny. People don't usually say the things I want them to.

Kim is coming back here after she's done babysitting. The kids live near me on the Upper East Side, as does Ben. I love that she's hanging out with me so much in general, but especially now while I'm so down. I do worry that I'll fall back into the habit of spending every available minute with her, though, as we did in the three years before we stopped being friends for six months. We resumed our friendship only a few weeks ago. I called her, and we talked about the fight we'd had. It's pretty uneventful. We just realized that we have little quarrels, and that it gets really bad when we let them escalate. Our plan is to not let that happen this time around. This degree of level-headedness is only achievable when sex and money aren't involved.

So today I am hanging out with Kim, who loves me. Later, I'm seeing John, who loves me. Tomorrow, my mother is coming from New Jersey, to love me. Is it wrong for me to make certain I never have any alone-time with me, who might not love me that much? Maybe it's good. Maybe I can heal while in the presence of others. *Because of their presence even.* Do I have to be by myself to heal and progress? I think, and hope, not because all that painful dealing-with-shit-on-my-own is not an option right now. I'm not up for it. *So* not up for it. You'll note, I have still not revealed the reason why I believe Ben and I are not together, but now I don't feel like it. Probably I should write it now because of how much I don't feel like it—like it might provide some kind of breakthrough. But fuck it, I'll have that breakthrough another time.

Now I'm dreading seeing John. I think that part of it is the simple fact that I don't feel like entertaining anyone except Kim and my mom and people like that—well actually, just Kim and Mom.

Kim kind of *is* Mom in that she's maternal and not that she is so similar to my mother, because she is not. How offended would Mom be if she read this? Mom, she's not *more* maternal than you are. How will Kim feel when she *does* read this, which she definitely will, since I'll ask her to. She may be flattered. Are you, Kim? I'll let you know what she says and I'm sure it won't be censored since, lately, she can't say a fucking word to me without having me enter it into this journal or story or whatever this is. That must be annoying for her. I'm sure I am a challenging friend to have right now: needy, completely self-absorbed and with no respect for anyone else's privacy. I'm not changing now though, I'm on a roll.

Feeling as I do now, I reflect up on the various times I have broken men's hearts and marvel at how remorseless I was, and still am, even though I am now experiencing that which I inflicted upon them. That is not to say I'm *glad* they were hurt, it's just like, "Well, that's them and their pain, and nothing matters to me but how I feel."

I don't really know what caused Ben to change his mind, but I don't think it matters much. What counts is that he feels differently. Could last night have been different? What if I had allowed myself to cry? What if I had tried to talk about all the good things we had—things we never had with other people? What if I had begged him? But begged him to what, feel like he did in the beginning? What if I had tried to reason with him, pointed out to him that only two weeks ago we were the happiest couple in the world? What if I'd gone for the dating-other-people option? Maybe it wouldn't have lasted too long before we went back to dating each other exclusively. Could it have been different and would it necessarily have been a good thing if it had?

One comforting thought: The fact that Ben broke up with me makes me feel like maybe he's not the soulmate I took him for. If we were so compatible, wouldn't we have stayed together? Would my actual soulmate break up with me? I don't know. What's nice is, at least for the time being, I'm getting a bit bored with the whole thing. I'm just going in circles, and that can only last so long. Another happy thought is that, in spite of the fact that all this musing over what could've saved the relationship is beginning to bore me, I am still miserable, have no appetite, and will probably lose those ten or so pounds I've been meaning to for the past five years. It's not a good way to lose weight, but for me, sorrow really does the trick. Ben was allergic to the cats anyway. I can't part with Kitty and Kat.

Kim just walked in. She brought me flowers and read this and liked it. Now she is going to read my tarot cards.

# MORNING #2

JOHN CAME OVER WHILE KIM was still here, and she read his tarot cards, too. When she left, he and I went out to dinner, and I paid for my half since that's how our relationship has always been. But I am less liberal and less liberated with each passing day, and it makes me sort of sick. It did before too, but I'm not as tolerant now since Ben never let me pay for anything. But then, Ben probably has more money. And in the grand scheme of things, my relationship with Ben has cost me far more.

I came to an interesting realization this morning: I'm progressing nicely through Elizabeth Kubler-Ross' stages of mourning. Of course, I am referring to death in the figurative sense with regard to this break-up. So the first stage—denial and isolation. Did that. Did the what-the-fuck-happened? the how-can-this-be?, the how-can-he-not-call?, and the will-he-ever-call? In fact,

he *did* call and likely would not have had it been his actual death that I was mourning. I felt lonely and iso-
lated.

But this morning I awoke to stage two—anger. I'm
not completely done with stage one yet, because every
time the phone rings I still hope it's him and I still miss
him terribly, but now I'm furious. I think about what he's
throwing away and how childish and selfish he is, how in-
capable he is of sharing and weathering the rough times,
and how at the first sign of cold feet he was out of there.
And I think, What a fucking waste of time to have loved
him. I'm not sure I buy that "it's better to have loved and
lost" shit, because here I am feeling significantly worse
than if I had never known him, and I don't find reflecting
on the good times we shared any comfort whatsoever.
Just the opposite.

I just read in my sociology book that the third stage
of death is bargaining, "in which the dying person makes
an agreement to die willingly if God or fate will allow him
or her to live a little longer." That kind of sucks, doesn't
it? How is that going to manifest itself? Can I pray that
we get back together for just a little while longer, or do I
have to call Ben and beg him? Is that bargaining? I am
not doing that. That stage is out. Anyway, I don't want
to get back together if we're destined just to break up
again. I could have agreed to see other people, which
would've been the same to me as a break-up, just more

painful and drawn out. But maybe I should've.

Before we dated exclusively, we were seeing other people and Ben didn't seem to be doing much about it. We still talked all the time. He was always available to talk or hang out. I don't think he was really dating anyone else, I just think he liked the idea of having his freedom. Should I give him that? Obviously, he has it now. But should I try to remain in his life? I don't know if I can. I'm not sure he'd want me to, and I'm not sure I see us dating other people as anything but a painful and degrading compromise on my part. Anyway, I'm at the anger stage so I don't have to worry about that now.

There are two more stages after bargaining: depression and acceptance. My book notes that "most people do not experience the stages in strict sequence. . .sometimes shifting between moments of hope and moments of despair." That Kubler-Ross said a mouthful. This sucks. Sometimes I really don't give a shit and think that how I feel about what's happening is completely within my power. I can choose to wallow in self-pity or, almost cheerfully, acknowledge that, when push comes to shove, I'm not one of those people who believes there's only one perfect mate out there, and so I will simply have to find another. No easy task, I admit, but my point is that I do firmly believe that a happy life and fulfilling relationship can be had with someone besides Ben.

At least I didn't eat much yesterday. That's something good. Stupid how I did it: lots of coffee, cigarettes, and Valium all day until around 8:00 p.m., when I had dinner with John. I had a glass and a half of white wine, two pieces of fried chicken, and some mashed potatoes. The chicken was so crispy that John and I joked that we weren't sure if we were eating well-fried chicken or just bones. At one point, his mouth full and mid-chew, he stopped one of the waiters and asked him, "Is this a bone in my mouth?" The guy was surprised and asked him to repeat the question. John, having asked solely for my amusement, blushed and quickly changed it to, "Are there any extra napkins?" which was also funny since there was already a pile of them on our table.

I have a prescription for Valium 10 mg tablets. What I like to do is break them into quarters or even eighths and just take like a little at a time, so that it's not a strong reaction I have, just a slight, steady calm all day long. Sometimes, Kim takes them with me. At some point yesterday evening, before John came, we discussed what we had been eating, and I said, "I haven't had any food yet, but I've been nibbling on these Valium all day." I love that I make her laugh, and that she is also very funny and so accepting of me.

Before John left at around 11:30 last night, he asked, "You're not into me anymore, are you? Like, I know you *like* me, but you're not into it, right?"

I do think he's right, but I pointed out that it has only been a day since Ben and I broke up, and that I'm still sad, and fairly heavily sedated, and one evening should not be a litmus test for the path our relationship will take.

It must've been a bummer for him, since when I left him for Ben, I tried to show, and genuinely felt, some remorse but was clearly excited about this new development in my life. And now that Ben is gone and John is back, it wasn't, I guess, the reunion he'd hoped it would be. But I never pretended I was leaving him for someone I "sort of" liked. He knew how strong my feelings for Ben had become, but he probably thought, now that Ben is out of the picture, we could pick up where we left off and things would be great. I don't see that happening but I can't say for certain that they won't. But they won't. I don't know why I liked John so much more before I loved Ben and why I feel so indifferent to him now. Maybe I am just letting his hopes or expectations influence me into thinking something is wrong with me. Or maybe it really *is* too soon.

My mother is coming in from New Jersey. Oh, speaking of my mother, I just realized there's another reaction I'm having to this break-up with Ben—shame and embarrassment.

Everyone knew that we were going out, and that I was spending all my time with him, and now I have to tell everyone that we're not together. And I feel very exposed and ashamed—like they all know I failed at something, or that bad feeling you get when everyone knows things are lousy for you. Like I wish I had never mentioned Ben to anyone, especially in such glowing terms. Now they'll all know it's over, if I tell them, and ultimately, even if I don't. And I don't know why it bothers me but it dies. *Does*. I typed *dies*. What dies? The relationship or the shame? Presumably they both go away sooner or later, so I guess this typo need not be exhaustively analyzed.

I wonder if Ben is thinking about me even half as much as I'm thinking about him. Of course he's not. He's probably not thinking about me at all. But if he is, I wonder what his thoughts are. I hate him. I hate him for making me think about him so much. But then, I think that I am thinking about him by my own choosing. And it's not at *all* because I hate him. So maybe it's good that I am thinking about him, so that I can work through this and get it, and him, out of my system.

Then I think there's a fine line between working through something, which is good, and obsessing about it, which is bad, and I don't want to do that. But it's only been two days, so I don't think that I am actually at the obsessing stage yet. (That's my own stage, not one of Kubler-Ross's: the obsessing stage. I've sort of spent my life in it. Self-indulgent and detached. I can't say that is entirely true, but it certainly is a little.)

Now I have to go to work. I have an ad running in

today's *Voice* for a studio apartment.

Guess what? Turns out I don't have to go to work today! I just got a call from Mom from the road. Car phone, *dahling*. She's halfway here. She asked if I would be home when she arrived, and I told her that I'd like to be, and she said, "Great!"

So I am not going to work because I feel I have her tacit permission not to. Isn't that the sickest thing, like, I don't work at all for my own gratification or for the money, I just do it because I am twenty-seven and my parents tell me I should. So I do, sometimes.

Now I am so happy that I don't have to go to the office. It's like having a snow day, except that most of my life is like that. I basically try to avoid responsibility as best I can except for when I get an idea about some business venture— like that Learning Annex course I would be genuinely excited to teach, until they tell me I can, at which point I'd likely lose all interest. I've joked with Kim about how I would probably show up late for the first class, unprepared, make some jokes, and never show up again. I can't count how many graduate schools I've dropped out of since college. I start taking a class, spend a shitload of Mom and Dad's money to enroll, complete the first two assignments, get A's, of course, and then, around the middle of the semester, get bored or overwhelmed and stop going. Obviously, I'm not proud of this behavior, but I am being honest.

I have to straighten up the apartment a bit and go get

that disgusting flavored cream Mom likes for her coffee, but first I'll recount the discussion we had. It's just like every other discussion we have, and because of that, it's priceless:

Mom: Sweetheart!

Me: (Probably less cheerful-sounding but feeling equally enthused) Hi.

Mom: Will you be home when I get there?

Me: (Trying to gauge from her question if she'll be angry or even know that "being home" means I blew off work today) I say, hopefully, "I'd like to."

Mom: Great! Then here's what we'll do. I'll come, put the car in the garage. . .do you have coffee and that good cream?

Me: (Lying about the cream but on my way out to get some) Yes.

Mom: OK, so I'll come and we'll have a cave day.

Me: What kind of day?

Mom: You know. . .a cave day. We'll stay home and hang out, and this evening we'll order in Thai food. Are you in the mood for Thai food?

Me: (Too comforted by my mother's voice and the prospect of spending the day doing nothing and doing it with her) Sounds great!

Mom: How was your date with John last night?

Me: Fine. I kind of don't give a shit, you know?

Mom: I know. Maybe don't date for a while.

Me: I really shouldn't.

Mom: Well, how's David?

That's my dry doctor who's Jewish and brilliant and would be perfect for me if he weren't so fucked up. He's a workaholic, can't commit, and there's that weird sex-guilt thing—especially unfortunate because his penis is perfect. Such a waste.

Me: Oh, Mom, I can't. You know I would if I could.

Mom: (Laughing and understanding) I hear you. Shame though. How about we write up an ad for New York Magazine? I'll put it on my card. It'll be my treat.

Me: Mom, I'll just meet losers. Nothing good will happen.

Mom: You never know. And I'm paying for it. What can you lose?

Me: I guess.

Then there were the "I love you's" and the "drive carefully," and now I have to go buy the gross cream.

MOM'S HERE! SHE LOVES THE CHANGES I've made to the apartment. I recently wallpapered and carpeted the small private foyer off the elevator all by myself. I hung the paper and laid the carpet, and the process was really enjoyable, and I think it even looks good. I was going for a kind of French country motif—warm, woodsy, welcoming. The little entry leads directly to my apartment, so there's no one else to object to my choices. And I saved money on labor by doing it myself, but I really did it because I thought it would be rewarding, and also because I hired a professional to wallpaper a different room in the apartment and he did a shitty job. I thought, I don't really know how to do this but, if I did, I could easily do it better than this guy. I didn't pay him hundreds of dollars just so he could leave wrinkles, bubbles, and even some rips in my fabulous Schumacher paper.

Mom's arrival brings about a wave of haughtiness which generally subsides soon after she leaves. Sometimes it's kind of fun caring about luxurious things and brand names, etc. Mom is elegant. She's Zsa Zsa-ish. It's all "dahling," "sweetie," and "lovey." Things are "to die for." She reminds me a bit of Eddie from *Absolutely Fabulous*, except that she's loving and supportive and doesn't insult me or resent me—as far as I know—for cramping her style or stealing her youth. She mostly wears black or beige and says she cannot even walk in a flat shoe. She has her hair done weekly, and none of us even knows what color it really is, including Mom. I have often described her as a Jewish Jackie O. But when it's just us, we chainsmoke, play hours and hours of poker and gin rummy, and curse like sailors. I am happy she's here.

Mom read my "dramatic monologue" and liked it but asked how I managed to seem so together if this is how I'm feeling inside. I was shocked that she thought I seemed together in the first place. I pointed out that most of what she read I'd written immediately prior to and promptly following the break-up when I was feeling my most sad and unstable. She was disgusted by the parts where I contemplated begging Ben to take me back or considered having an open relationship with him. Of course, she's protective of me. She said, "Yeah, me too," when she read the part about Kim wanting to call Ben to tell him off.

One thing I didn't understand was how she did not know that I am terribly insecure, filled with self-doubt, and, at the same time, a self-centered egomaniac. I was surprised that she was surprised. Hadn't she known this about me? I am the smartest, sexiest, funniest, prettiest woman alive, but I am also a needy, lazy, self-indulgent, neurotic loser. Sometimes I feel one way, sometimes the other. Usually both. I was also surprised that, even if she hadn't known that I was this kind of person, how could she not understand, at least, that there could *be* this kind of person. It's like it was a new concept for her. Isn't everyone intensely self-confident, cocky, and at least sometimes, simultaneously crippled by self-loathing and doubt? I guess not. Or maybe they are but not to this extent.

Mom's happy about my break-up. She thinks I should be with someone more mature, grounded, employed, and marriage-minded. She knew—because I told her—about the beginning, how at first Ben didn't want to be in a serious relationship, and that he doesn't want kids, and that he'd never had a girlfriend. I hate hearing her criticize him, but it is helpful. What *was* I thinking? What am I *still* thinking, because I'm not really done feeling like this is the best relationship I've ever had, at least in a long time. I guess it's just hard when you're not on the same page with someone whose company you really enjoy.

# MORNING #3

T'S 8:05 A.M., AND I HAVE TO GO TO WORK—and I *really* have to, because yesterday, from home, I arranged to meet a bunch of people at an apartment and my first appointment is at 9:00 a.m. So I'm going to work. I will just say quickly that, this morning when I woke up, I felt a bit like I could envision Ben becoming little more than a vague memory. . .like, just another guy I've dated and then not dated.

Is this exciting? Is it too soon to feel this way? Am I denying or repressing my hurt? Does this mean I never truly loved him? I mean, it's only Morning #3, and I'm already grateful to the kid for not wasting more of my time. It never would have worked in the long run; it was just lots of fun, so much fun, and now he's mercifully (not by design, of course) freed me to pursue a more appropriate, less fun relationship.

What a fool I'll feel like having written this if we get back together. And I'll admit that part of me wants to and part of me, maybe the bigger part, I'm not sure, just wants him to want to. Not in that spiteful way, like I want him to come crawling back so I can be mean and say "no," just in that way that wants to be wanted. But, of course, there's also some spite. I must get dressed.

I WENT TO WORK, AND NOW IT'S 4 P.M. and I'm home. Had lunch with Mom and Kim. It's the first time they've hung out since I had my fight with Kim. It was nice that we could all do something together, particularly since Kim's mother just died about a month ago and Mom is very huggy and kissy with Kim and thinks she's wonderful. Kim's mother was the opposite, but that's another story. Then Kim came back home with me and read more of the story.

I think there's something odd about my calling these journal entries "a story" and not merely permitting, but really *encouraging*, everyone to read them. These are my innermost thoughts, essentially my diary, yet I feel removed and treat them like they're a paper I might be working on for a class or something. It's like I'm soliciting feedback for a confession. Why? Do I want to be forgiven for my sins? Maybe I want to be punished?

Did I mention that Ben called yesterday and left a message on the machine? Just, "Hey, give me a call." I didn't pick up, and I've decided to screen every call and not contact him for I don't know how long, if ever. At some point I would like to get my stuff back. I left some clothes, contact lenses, games, and discs at his place. Mom says not to call, and that she'll replace everything, but I feel like these are my things and there's no reason why I shouldn't get them back.

I'm worried, though, that if I call him, a woman might answer the phone. Not because I think he was cheating, though he absolutely might have been, but more because he doesn't hesitate to have strange women stay over and also answer his phone. When we first started dating, he would ask me to get the phone if he was in the bathroom or going out to walk his dogs. And this was in the very beginning! Also, I worry that the only reason he called yesterday was to ask me when I'll be picking up my things. Not that they take up so much space, but maybe he just wants them out. But I don't think that's why he called. I also don't think he called to get back together. I think he just likes me and wants to stay friends.

Mom pointed out something interesting with regard to the timing of the break-up. Ben and I had just gone together to get tested for HIV. We were negative, and the next step was going to be that I would go on the pill or get a diaphragm. When she said it could have to do with my going on the pill, I thought she meant that Ben had gotten nervous because it symbolized too much of a commitment for him, or that it meant he couldn't then risk having unprotected, or really even protected, sex outside the relationship without possibly jeopardizing my life. Because, you know, condoms aren't a hundred percent protection against diseases.

Instead, her point was that he might have been worried that I would only pretend to go on birth control in order to get pregnant to trap him into marriage. That he might fear this would never have *occurred* to me. I would never do something like that. I guess there are girls who would, but those are not the circumstances under which I want to start a family, and I don't think I could've gotten him that way anyway. He couldn't force me to abort but he could refuse to marry me, and I think he would have.

It's just amazing. I wonder if this was a factor. I doubt I'll ever find out because I'll probably never have the chance to ask him, and I doubt he would even admit it if it were the case. I'll bet it's even a possibility that he felt this way on some unconscious level and wasn't aware of it. It is interesting, though, because I admit I was totally pushing for the test so that we wouldn't have to use rubbers. Sex is so much better without them. Maybe that made him feel like I was pressuring him because I had some ulterior motive. But then why did he get the test with me? He even made the appointment. It could just be that he wanted to make sure we were both healthy. Or maybe he was keen on the idea of the pill but then got suspicious, or a friend or relative of his warned him that I might be up to something. Who the fuck knows? There's no use speculating.

I am bored of talking about Ben. Actually, I don't think I've really been talking about him much at all, it's just that I'm writing about him, and our break-up, every chance I get. I haven't stopped writing since I started shortly before he came over to end things.

This might be the most I've written since my college thesis which was, by the way, "A Psychoanalytic Interpretation of Shakespeare's *King Lear* and *A Midsummer Night's Dream*." I got an A on that, thank you very much. It was the most fun I had working on something for school. I loved college except for the classes and the homework. Like the way I love the beach except for the ocean and the sand. I didn't do very well as a result. I got by, though, and it didn't take me more than four years, with a summer class here and there. It was an Ivy, too. I wish I had made better use of my time there.

Ben didn't finish college. And it's a mediocre college he didn't finish. And he's never had a job. And he's about my height and kind of plump. And the worst part is that none of these things actually matters to me and there's no sense in talking about them as if they make him a loser, because they don't. He's brilliant and funny and handsome and just unable to commit right now. I like to think that he's emotionally unavailable in general, because it hurts much more to think it has to do with me specifically.

But it really is also genuinely plausible, since he's never had a serious relationship with anyone before me. So it's not like he gets seriously involved with every woman he dates. In fact, I was the exception.

From virtually every relationship, I've kept something tangible. Often they're your standard gifts like cards, love letters, jewelry, souvenirs, and such. And I'm the kind of person who'll generally save things for sentimental reasons, but one particular thing I notice I always keep—it usually starts off as something I borrow—is an old boyfriend's jeans or some denim article of clothing. I still have a denim shirt from Sam, the controlling business school student I dated my freshman year of college. I have the beat-up jeans I wouldn't let Seth (much older, successful, comedy producer, sophomore and junior year) throw out. He was wearing them the New Year's Eve when we had sex in Carly Simon's closet, so they're a fun memento. I have a pair of Andrew's (senior year) jeans. Okay, the shirt I have of David's (dry doctor) is flannel. And now I have a pair of Ben's jeans.

And I don't just keep these things, I *wear* them. And all these men were different sizes and shapes, but still, everything fits. I know there must be some symbolism to the taking of the clothes. Not that I just *take* them, it generally happens that I've slept over, was wearing some tiny sexy thing the night before, and in the morning I want to change into something more comfortable and casual.

They offer me jeans and either tell me I can keep them or I just get attached to them and over time they become mine. I think there's meaning in that it's something that belonged to them, something they never formally gifted to me, something that they wore, and that they're of relatively little monetary value. I'd much rather remember Seth while wearing his jeans than by wearing the expensive necklace he gave me, as beautiful as it is. And denim gets all beat up and even cozier over time, and it's outlasted even my longest relationship.

# MORNING #4

STILL BUMMED BUT FEELING MUCH BETTER. It does bother me that it's Friday, and I assume Ben will go out to the Hamptons and have a blast with his friends from the house and probably fool around with someone, but that's not even a big deal, it's just the idea of him sunning himself by the pool and hanging with his pals and being not the least bit bothered by our break-up. In fact, he's probably psyched that he's free to do whatever he wants. At first, I was particularly annoyed that he has the luxury of leaving the city on weekends. When he's not at his place on the Upper East Side, he must be even less inclined to think about me, since that's where we both live and used to hang out together. But now I realize that I, too, could go away for a weekend. I could go to my friend Liz's Hampton share, though I'm not sure she'd have room, and I probably wouldn't really wanna go anyway since she's the only one I'd know there. Or I could visit my parents in New Jersey, but that's often a little depressing for some reason, probably because it's Atlantic City and I can't take too much of there, or them.

Last night I went over to Liz and her husband's place for dinner. We got together because we're sort of friends (Liz works in my real estate office) and also because she and her husband are both lawyers and we wanted to discuss the possibility of forming a corporation. Amy, another friend from work, suggested we approach Liz with the idea that we all leave our office and Amy and I would work for Liz, who, as a lawyer, automatically has her broker's license. As agents not yet eligible for brokers' licenses, Amy and I have to be employed by a broker. We give our broker, Sam, a major percentage of our commission, and he argues that it's fair because "I have all this overhead, and I pay for your advertising and phones and desks and use of the fax and copier, and other things like that." But Amy pointed out that, if we pay for all that stuff ourselves, maybe Liz, or some other broker, would be willing to take a significantly smaller cut.

Amy couldn't make it last night, so I went anyway and proceeded to get drunk on the wine we sipped before, during, and after dinner. And I already have no head for business, so I'm sure it was not as productive as it could've been. At least I left with all of us enthusiastic about the possibility of working together and making lots of money, and with Liz's husband, Rob, offering to research what needs to be done and what would be the next step. I am more scared than happy. I'm scared of failing. I'm scared of getting screwed by two lawyers even if they are my friends. I'm scared of having to work as hard as I expect I would have to if we are starting our own business. But I am excited, too. We shall see.

I keep recalling this one time when Ben was over and I told him about this varicose vein I have on the back of my leg. I had known vaguely that it was there, but I hadn't really noticed, until I was in the dressing room at Ann Taylor trying on a short skirt, how pronounced it is. He asked to see it. I was embarrassed—even though I was the one who brought it up—and I was like, "No, you *really* don't want to see this. No one should have to see this."

I was joking about it and wouldn't show it to him and he said, "Jess, I am going to see you when your tits are down to your knees, you've got liver spots everywhere, and your pussy hair's all white and nasty, so let's see it." So I showed it to him and he immediately said, "I think we should see other people."

And when I first thought about this incident, all I could think about was the fact that he seemed, at least then, to have every intention of spending his life with me. But now that I write about it, is there something to his hilarious reaction? I don't think so, but maybe? We were getting along so well then. I think that's what I find so painful. We just assumed we'd be together when we were old. At least I did. How can he have been so in love and then suddenly not? So abruptly, with no provocation (other than the vein) that I know of. Was it all talk? But he never talked like that to anyone else. His mom even told me so. When we went out to dinner at Caviarteria, even though I wore that way too short dress that made me look more cheap than sexy, his mom said Ben had never spoken of any girl as highly as he had of me. She said she could tell even before meeting me that I was special. It was probably my one shot at actually liking a potential mother-in-law.

Which of Kubler-Ross's stages is this? The confusion stage? I should be in therapy. I need help, and I have to go to work. I have to show that damn studio until I rent it. I thought about roller skating over there, but I'm sort of dizzy. Also, I feel like I'm running out of things to say. Life just sucks right now. I know it won't always suck, and if I could just immerse myself in my work, I'd be distracted and making money, and I'd feel much better about myself.

GLAD THAT'S OVER. I went to work. It was totally uneventful. Three of my four appointments stood me up, and the one who showed wanted something bigger. Fuck that—what do they think they're going to get for $850 a month? I should never have taken this listing as an exclusive. But I fuck the building's owner sometimes, and I can't turn down the crappy apartments since he also gives me great ones from time to time.

It's much easier to blow him than when he wants to fuck. A blowjob can happen quickly in his car, just parked someplace secluded along Riverside Drive or somewhere, but when he wants to get laid, he comes to my apartment for "lunch." And it's a whole production, since he's like sixty-five and it takes him forever with the condom, and then he has to shower so his wife doesn't smell anything "off" when he gets home. I think his wife is the one who owns all the buildings, but his father was big in New York City politics many years ago. No one knows about us besides Kim and Amy. Mom would be appalled even though she might have done the same. Or not. I think she once told me a story about her father being very sick when she was single, and that they couldn't afford his medication, so she had some "arrangement" with the pharmacist. Of course, that was in an effort to save her father's life, which admittedly is very different from my situation, in which it's just easier to blow the landlord than sit in the office making cold calls to try to drum up leads. My boss doesn't actually know, but he suspects. And he makes jokes like, "Don't you have anything nicer to wear for your meeting?" And he does the air quotes with his fingers when he says "meeting." Needless to say, I never mentioned the reason behind my exclusive apartments to Ben. Ben would probably not care, even when he loved me; he probably would have found it amusing or irrelevant but he might have acted like it was bad as a way to guilt or shame me. Or for leverage. That's just what couples do.

Amy was in the office when I got in. We went to a bar, and I had a vodka and orange juice and she just had juice. I felt a little like an alcoholic, drinking in the afternoon, but she smokes pot every day, so I didn't feel completely deviant—as if it's OK for me to be fucked up if she is also. Why should her problems justify or diminish mine? Of course they shouldn't, but they do.

One good thing, I told Amy about Ben and my breaking up, and she was totally indifferent, and even though that's just because she's so unhappy and self-absorbed, it somehow made me feel better. If she hadn't treated it so nonchalantly, I might have worked myself back into thinking, *It's so tragic, I'm so sad.* But receiving no sympathy from her made it seem like no big deal, which is how I want to view it. Sometimes the more sympathy and support I have, the worse I handle things. The way you're not supposed to make a huge deal about your kid just scraping their knee or something. If I am forced to cope on my own, I am much stronger and more stable.

At some point she said, "Well, now I can tell you that I never thought he was right for you." I asked her if she really meant it or if she was just saying it to make me feel better.

"No way, man," she said. "I would just never have told you that when you were with him."

"But why?" I asked her. "It might have given me some perspective. I'd have appreciated it."

"Ohhhhh, *no! People never want to hear that kind of thing when they're in love," she said, cynically, and wisely.

My friend Abigail has said the same thing, that there's no use talking to someone about their relationship while they're in it, that they just resent you and think you're wrong and jealous. I disagree. I think you shouldn't badger a friend to end a relationship you consider unhealthy, but it's not bad to say something if you phrase it tactfully. I think that either Amy and Abigail had friends who took well-intentioned comments badly, or, more likely, they are the kind of people who don't want anyone to burst their bubble so they project this onto everyone else.

Then I asked her, eagerly, to tell me exactly what she thought was wrong with my relationship with Ben.

> Amy: It just wouldn't have worked. It just wasn't right.
>
> Me: "Oh, come on," I begged, desperate to hear her criticize him. . .to make me feel less at a loss without him. "You say that for *some* reason. What about it seemed wrong to you?"
>
> Amy: Well, he wasn't working, and you weren't working, and you just kept each other company. It was convenient. It's not like he had anything to offer

you. He's not half as sharp or quick-witted as you are. You would have tired of him if he hadn't ended it.

I was comforted by the thought that maybe all Ben and I were really doing was keeping each other company, but I was disheartened by the part about him not being all that smart, because Amy had only met him briefly and really he is quite able to hold his own in terms of witty banter and clever conversation, she just didn't get to see that side of him. The problem with her saying it was not that I was angry or felt protective of him, it was that it made me question the extent to which *any* of her assessment was correct. I wanted her to be spot-on with all of her observations, so I could trust that she knew of what she spoke. But that's not entirely reasonable or necessary because:

1. It's not her job to help me get past this. It's mine.
2. It's not from thinking Ben is worthless or stupid that I'm going to get over this, because he's not.
3. She can be right about some things and not others.

I feel compelled to address the fact that all I have done for the past few days, every chance I get, is write. It's become like an addiction, a drug. I don't know what to make of it. It seems to be more of a need than a decision. Like, when you're exhausted and don't intend to fall asleep but just do and are surprised when you wake up, the way I am sometimes surprised to find myself at this computer typing, or surprised when I notice that I've been going at it for hours, or surprised by how much I've written.

I wonder why I am doing it. I have never used writing this way before. In the past, if things were going particularly well, or poorly, I might keep a journal, but it was always erratic and never with this kind of fervor or consistency. Is this a good thing? Why must I question everything?

This is actually quite out of the ordinary for me and, at the very least, worth noting if not questioning. I think it's part of my whole trying-to-better-understand-myself-and-the-world-around-me thing. It may even have very little to do with Ben. He may have just been the catalyst because, long before Ben, I was interested in tarot cards and went, prior to any involvement with him, to a Buddhist meeting with Amy, who has been practicing for eight years. I have always been interested in self-exploration.

I love that I am writing. I think it's healthy. But as it is so like me to fear and question, I also worry that I am using it to withdraw from the rest of the world. Maybe the writing is not good but an excuse not to participate in life. Conversely, I worry that the writing *is* good and, like so many other projects I've begun, I will give up and abandon it at some crucial point. But then, maybe I'll abandon it when it stops serving its function, when I've gotten all I can from it, and in fact it will be the right thing to do, to stop. I can't believe I give this much thought to every little thing. It's a wonder I can function at all with all this. . . what does my shrink call it? *Ruminating.*

Anyway, I'm not going to stop writing until I do. Does that make sense? I mean, I'm not going to overanalyze it. I'm just going to go with it. This should be the worst addiction I ever have. It certainly beats drinking, taking pills, having bad relationships, *et cetera.*

And if I am withdrawing from life for a time, that might not be such a bad thing. So what? I can go through stages. I do not have to be the epitome of consistency. This is what I need to do right now. Why? I don't know. I suspect the answer is clear to everybody but me. I always feel that my problems and actions are totally textbook, but that I simply haven't got the background in psychology or the objectivity to know what's really going on.

That's one of the difficulties I have with therapy. I know I'm supposed to figure things out for myself but I'm always just sitting there thinking, Come on, you know you read about this very behavior and its causes in Psych 101, so let's just cut to the chase. It's interesting that I would feel so textbook and simultaneously so unique. But then, I feel like that too must be some textbook way of thinking, that there is some clinical term for that feeling or for the kind of person who has it—the clinical term for "individual feels totally unique and totally ordinary at the same time."

This might not be productive, this constant questioning. I just don't know how to stop. And then, of course, there is the question of whether or not *to* stop questioning. I feel I can rationalize anything, like I don't know right from wrong and good from bad. Of course, I am not talking about the *obvious*, like is it bad to kill people or to hurt oneself or others. Although that too can be a situation-specific gray area. I mean, the way I don't know if writing incessantly is good or bad. I can choose to view it as either. Or the way I don't know if I really cared that much for Ben or just make myself believe I did. Or didn't. Today I am leaning toward the belief that the relationship was a superficial one and just fun for the time being. Do I really feel this way, or am I simply comforted by adopting this viewpoint? In reality, how comforting is it to think that someone fun doesn't love you and is no longer in your life? Isn't fun the goal?

Sometimes it concerns me how, out of pride or insecurity, I can just totally write someone out of my life.

Wait! *Write someone out of my life?* Is that what I am doing, literally writing Ben out of my life? Is that why I have been writing incessantly? How I love having stumbled onto this— what? Metaphor? Analogy? Pun? But it is bad too, because if that is what I'm doing, and I'm working so hard (as I said before, *incessantly*) to do it, doesn't that mean I must have cared for Ben a great deal?

I would rather not think of things this way. Maybe it's not really Ben I'm ridding myself of but what he represents: losing myself in a relationship, focusing all my time and emotional energy on another person, basing so much of my self-worth on someone else's opinion of me. Maybe it's not my love for Ben that keeps me up at night writing but my love of self, or the love I'm trying to feel for myself. I'm writing out, not Ben, but the part of me that causes unhappy situations like Ben to happen. I'm writing him out and writing me in. Fuck, who knows, maybe I just loved the guy.

I would like to feed this story into an automated therapist and get back an assessment or reading. What I would *really* like is a crystal ball. I don't want to spend any more time or money with some shrink, as has virtually always been the case, who will let me just sit around and talk about nothing and get nowhere, or make only temporary strides only to revert back to my original way of behaving.

I have a therapist now whom I like because he lets me come whenever I want and doesn't pressure me into coming regularly, and because he's brilliant and confrontational and will tell me things and make statements instead of just asking questions. He also writes me prescriptions for anything I want. Plus he's gorgeous. His approach is an unconventional one. He once told me that a colleague of his had made mention of him to another psychiatrist and the second doctor, who didn't know my shrink but knew of him, asked, "Is that the guy who yells at his patients?" And it is. I have sat in his office bored and fidgeting, only to have him say, "Do you think *I* want to be here right now?" Like it was no picnic for him either. Once I talked to him for forty-five minutes nonstop, mostly about The Blue Oyster Cult, and at the end of the session I said, "I feel kind of guilty for not letting you get a word in edgewise."

He replied, "Don't you think I'd have interrupted if I had something to say?" I love a straight shooter.

# MORNING #? . . . 5

THINK IT'S GREAT NEWS THAT I had to scroll back to find out what morning this is, because it means that I am no longer keeping close track, at least in my head, of how long it's been since I last saw Ben.

Today is Saturday, and I have to go show that studio soon, and I can't say it doesn't bother me that, this being July 4th weekend, there's a good chance Ben won't be back in town until like Tuesday or Wednesday. Of course, there is a chance that he's in town now, but I doubt it.

And the problem with his being away is, as I mentioned before, that I know he'll be having a good time and not confronted by memories of me the way he might be at home. He's obviously not angst-ridden about memories of me anywhere he goes since he's the reason it's over. I don't know why I want him to be thinking about me, but I know it's natural to feel this way for whatever reason. I'm sure a lot of it is because I am thinking so much about him.

It seems to me that, while I may really have been, or may still be, in love with Ben, another factor is simply my desire to be in love with *someone*. And to be loved. I mourn the loss of *a* relationship as much as I mourn the loss of *that* relationship.

But I can't avoid giving Ben some credit. It was not merely readiness on my part, because other men I've dated recently have wanted to get more serious and I didn't want to. So it's not only a matter of timing. Ben is special. But at the same time, I do think that I seized, with Ben, upon what felt like the first viable relationship option in a long time. I don't want one if it's not right, but if it feels right, as it did, I want it all and right away. Historically, if I wasn't completely into a guy, like head over heels, I didn't want anything to do with him, but if I did manage to like someone, like Ben, then I thought, *I found the man I'm going to marry.* There's never any middle ground.

Last night I read to Mom the part about "writing" Ben out of my life. She liked it a lot. She noted, as I had known and witnessed over the years, that she is the same way. I have seen her be best friends with someone for years, and then something will happen and the friendship ends, and it's like that person barely even existed. And she can talk about the person—usually not even disparagingly, because she's not a grudge-holder—but matter-of-factly, like they're just someone or other and there's no mention of the fact that maybe this was her closest friend for decades or even anyone who had ever much mattered.

I am more this way with men than with women. When Kim and I had our fight, I still thought about it, and talked about it, and missed Kim. But I'll admit that, while I did want to be friends again, I wasn't really tempted to call until I was ready to call, and then I did.

With Ben, I am only tempted to have *him* call. And *so* tempted I am. I don't want to call him, but I do want my stuff that's at his place. With Kim, had she called, I would have welcomed her back. Whereas, if Ben calls, I won't answer the phone (screening) and probably won't return the call unless it relates to my belongings. I want the satisfaction of knowing he's thinking about, and trying to reach, me. I want Ben to want me back, but I don't know if I would actually go back to him if he asked me. I'm just so hurt.

Lately, I've been feeling like Ben is just this kid (he's twenty-three) who really hasn't got it to give right now. When we first started dating, he said he didn't want a relationship, and I guess I should've paid more attention to that. I mean, I didn't push for it. I said, "OK, I'm sorry you feel that way," and continued to date other people. But when he asked me to break up with the other men I'd been seeing, namely John, to go out exclusively with him, I did so immediately, and maybe I should have proceeded with more caution. But how can anyone know, except afterwards, with the benefit of hindsight, that letting oneself be vulnerable to another person is a mistake or ill-timed? I wouldn't feel foolish about it now if it had worked out, right? And too much caution can take the spark out of everything and make for so many missed opportunities.

From work today, I went over to the post office for my parents. They have a mailbox there. The post office is about three blocks from where Ben lives, and I thought, What if I see him? Now I feel I always want to look my best in case I bump into him. This is not only because I want to look great, so he'll want me back, but because I don't want to feel like some slovenly loser, if he's with one of those rich, Jappy women he dates—the ones whose nails are always manicured and who look really put together, even on the hottest and most humid of days. Then, too, it would bother me if he were with some really cute, kind of hippie-ish chick in cut-off jeans and a band T-shirt. Essentially, seeing him with any type of attractive woman would hurt me, especially if I didn't think I looked good that day.

On my way to the post office I thought that if I saw him, with or without a girl, and whether he did or did not see me, I would ignore him. Even if he called to me, I would have my earphones on and would pretend not to hear him. Then I thought, it would also be nice to walk over and punch him. Hard. In the face. But I would never really do anything like that. I actually find the thought repulsive. Yet nice, too.

Then I thought that I wish he would move away. But then I realized that I am lucky and it could be worse: What if we worked together or had mutual friends or something?

But I still wish he would move. Then I was reminded of the time that he and I were walking down the street and he pointed to a woman and said, "I had a date with her," very nonchalantly. And though they apparently only had one date, and he and I had some kind of relationship, I wondered would he refer to me as casually if he saw me now. Like, "I dated her," or "That girl and I went out," or "There's my old girlfriend." I hate him. I would like to avoid ever seeing him again.

Mom thinks I should forget about my stuff at his apartment. Do I want it back just so I have an excuse to get in touch with him? I don't know. I don't think so. But then I think that every time I think that I don't think something, it's probably because I really do and I am just in denial or selectively overlooking the obvious. I told Mom that I want, and feel entitled to, my possessions. Then she suggested I have Kim call to ask for them and have her pick them up from his doorman. I'm not sure Kim would do it, but my primary concern was that I would look silly doing that, or worse, I might seem even more upset than I really am, as if I can't even bear to do the most basic task if it involves Ben.

But lately, I kind of like the idea of having Kim call and be polite and just take care of it for me so I don't have to be bothered by any emotional bullshit or the prospect of having to see him. Maybe Kim's husband, Steve, would do it. Or maybe Kim would do it if Steve joined her. I will pose the question tonight.

Tonight, I'm having dinner with Kim, Steve, and Kim's dad in Chinatown. I really don't want to go because I don't want to do anything but be here in my apartment or in Kim and Steve's apartment, but mostly my apartment, because that way I can write, which is all I want to do. Kim bought me a present. I don't know what it is but it doesn't matter because it's just so sweet and so much the kind of thing Kim does, in general, and especially when I'm down.

She nagged me into going to dinner tonight. She said I should get out of the house, and when I told her I don't want to, she said I should force myself. I don't know if I exactly agree with that, but she said she and Steve will come back here after dinner if I want, and that was a big inducement. I don't like to leave the apartment, but I love when Kim and Steve visit. We drink wine and smoke pot (very little smoking for me, since it mostly makes me paranoid and hungry) and watch MMA or play video games. We love Donkey Kong and Mortal Kombat.

Mom thinks I should write, not just about Ben, but

about every boyfriend I've had. She said that it might be cathartic, and that I might gain insight into myself and see patterns I may, or may not, be repeating. I am not sure why this doesn't interest me. It just feels like such an undertaking. Such a lot of shit to dredge up. I don't feel up to it right now. Conversely, these entries do focus almost entirely upon Ben, and there were significant relationships in my life before him. It's just that this is the most recent and the one I feel most in need of addressing.

I had an interesting dream last night. It was night, and I was out with my high school friends Lisa and Abigail, but it was now, and though it was night, all the stores were open, and we, for some reason, decided to steal something. We were going to steal it—whatever *it* was I can't now recall, but I knew in the dream—but it was a specific smallish object. Anyway, I can't remember if we were going to steal it just to see if we could, or because it was valuable, and we were going to try to sell it and divide the money we got. So we were in the store, and then the lights got very dim and simultaneously the salesperson turned away from us and it was the perfect time, but I was afraid to take it, so I asked Abigail to grab it. It would've fit perfectly under her jacket. But she too chickened out, and we left. Then we were in my elevator, which is small, and there were two adorable cats that I assumed belonged to someone in my building, but I got the distinct impression that they had been abandoned or discarded. And there was a broken glass Coke bottle on the floor, and the soda had spilled out all around the shards of glass, and the cats were playing and rolling around near it. I realized that they could get hurt and I decided to take them home with me in spite of the fact that I already have Kitty and Kat. I told myself that they would simply have to adjust to two more animals. But then I saw, also in this tiny elevator, eight or ten little cages, each with a little puppy in it. The cages were stacked two rows high and four or five across, and they were on top of a high table so that I was at eye-level with the dogs. They all looked virtually the same, and all so small and pathetic. I decided that I couldn't take them all, but I had to take just one. And I was studying them to see which was the cutest. I was trying to imagine what they would look like full grown because all puppies are cute but not all dogs are. And interestingly, they all looked kind of like Ben's dogs—which I didn't think were that cute and which, by the way, were not housebroken, but I came to love them anyway because they were his and had sweet, loving dispositions.

# DAY #6

'M CALLING THIS "DAY" INSTEAD OF "MORNING" because I didn't start writing right away as I have for the past few days. It's about 5:30 p.m. Kim is over. She and Steve slept over, and we had brunch, but now he's back at their place working on a painting, and Kim stayed here with me. She's in the other room playing Nintendo. We had an eventful night last night. We went out to dinner in Chinatown and then to my place after picking up pot from their apartment and stopping by Blockbuster to rent Mortal Kombat II.

When we got home, there was a message on my machine from Abigail, to whom I have not mentioned the break-up because we've just been out of touch for the past week or so, and because I have been so busy writing about it that I had no energy to talk about it, too. Her message said: *Hi, Jessie, I just tried calling you at Ben's and—what's going on? Please call me as soon as you get this message.*

So I thought, Maybe Ben is away for the weekend but a woman is staying there and answered his phone. Or Ben is home for the weekend and a woman is there and answered his phone. Or Ben is at home, answered his own phone imitating a woman's voice, and told Abigail about the break-up. Something was definitely up because her message was filled with concern and confusion.

So I called her back while Kim and Steve played Nintendo and told her that Ben and I had broken up. I didn't go into too much detail because it's painful, and I feel ashamed (I mean, he dumped me), and also it's kind of boring me at this point, too. But I drilled her for information. "Okay, what *exactly* did he say when you called?" I was dying to hear every word, still searching for some insight.

"Well, he was just really surprised that I was calling. . . that I didn't know about the break-up. He said, 'Jess didn't tell you? We broke up.' And I was like, 'No! I had no idea.' Then he asked me when I last spoke to you and I told him Wednesday and he was like so surprised and said, 'That's so weird, because we were broken up then.' And I told him that I had invited you to a party and you said you had plans. . . ."

I think that was the night that I went over to Liz and Rob's.

"Then I told him that I said you should bring Ben to the party, and you said, 'I don't think Ben can make it,' but you hadn't said anything about breaking up. And he was like, 'Well, I've been calling and calling, and her machine is always on, and I don't know where she is, and I think she might be in Jersey but I don't wanna call there, and I've been really trying to track her down. Do you know where she is?' So I told him I didn't know where you were either, and he asked me to call as soon as I got in touch with you. He sounded really worried."

All this totally pissed me off because it seemed like he was worried that I might be suicidal or have gone into seclusion because I am so devastated. And even if this is just his ego talking, it still made me angry. It also made me angry because it wasn't that far-fetched. Also, he said he's been calling so much, but I only heard from him twice, the time when I was on the other line with Liz and called him back, and the time he left that brief message on my machine. So maybe he's been calling and hanging up a lot, which is annoying.

First, I asked Abigail to call him back and tell him I'm fine and not to worry about me.

She asked if she should lie and tell him that I got back together with John, and that we're really happy, and that I feel like we were meant to be together, etc. But I thought that was too childish and transparent. Then I asked her to get my stuff from his apartment for me. But then I realized I don't want her to call him and that he can go fuck himself. By the way, intellectually, I realize that he is completely allowed to change his mind about wanting a relationship with me and has actually not done anything wrong. But still.

Kim, overhearing my discussion, suggested that I write Ben a note asking for my things instead of involving other people. I agreed with that. So I begged Abigail not to call him back. I was afraid that she, thinking she's being really helpful and a great friend, might tell him that I'm really upset that she thinks we belong together or some shit. She promised not to call him and, if he got a hold of her, to just say, "Jess's fine."

Then another weird thing happened. Not long after my conversation with Abigail, Ben called and left a really curt message that sounded maybe angry, maybe frustrated. He said, "Jess, just return my call, please. Thank you."

And I freaked out because I thought Abigail must've called him and said, "Jess's home and not in New Jersey, and you should call her now!" So right after, at around 2:00 a.m.—Kim and Steve were still playing Mortal Kombat—I called Abigail again to ask if she had called Ben. And she swore, and I believe her, that she hadn't. So I was like, "Well, it's so strange," and she said maybe he had called me because he hadn't heard back from her and assumed that, had she tried to reach me and been unable, she might've been worried and would have called him. But since she hadn't called him back, he assumed, correctly, that she had gotten in touch with me and I am fine and just not returning his calls since I want him out of my life. Or, at least, I very much *want to want* him out of my life.

It was especially annoying because I don't want to have to keep being reminded of him. And I had really mixed feelings about the fact that Abigail had called him not knowing we'd broken up. Not that it was her fault. She didn't know.

But then I was horrified by the thought that maybe he thinks I put her up to it. Like, I had her call and just act surprised as some childish way of illustrating to him that I am too unaffected by our break-up to even mention it to friends. As if that's how inconsequential the relationship was to me. But that was pretty far-fetched, so I didn't worry about it for long.

Then I thought, hopefully, that maybe Ben actually believed that I didn't mention the break-up because I was, in fact, not heartbroken. Of course, I ended up thinking that he probably thinks I didn't tell her about it because it is so painful. That is most likely what he is thinking, and if so, unfortunately, he's not that far off from the truth.

# MORNING #7

MORE STUFF HAPPENED LAST NIGHT, but I couldn't write about all of it because Kim was getting bored playing Nintendo by herself. I could have asked her to go home, so I could write, but I love having her here. Anyway, the night before last, when I first spoke about all this shit to Abigail, I wrote Ben a letter:

> *Dear Ben,*
>     *Please send me the stuff I left at your place. There are some clothes, my contact lenses, and a few games.*
>                         *Thanks, Jess*

But I wrote it by hand and didn't type it, and that's exactly how it went. And it's mean, but I am so excited for him to get it because I know, when he sees the envelope, he'll definitely think there's more in store than just what it says. I'm totally psyched to not give him the satisfaction of—*anything.*

Also last night, I got another call from Abigail. She told me that Ben called her while she was out and left a message on her machine asking if she had contacted me and would she please call him back. I don't know what he's doing, because I realized that, if he were truly concerned about my safety or well-being, he could call my parents, even if he's uncomfortable doing so. And he could also come by my building and ask the doorman if I've been around, or if I am OK. Both these things would be fairly extreme, but if he thinks I am *that* devastated and he's really worried, they would be two simple solutions. So I don't know why he's calling Abigail. I don't think he's interested in her, so I think it's either just that he wants the dirt on how I am doing and if I'm back with John, or maybe it's just his way of staying in touch.

Once again I begged Abigail not to call him back, and she promised she wouldn't. But then she said, "What if he calls me and I pick up?" It is valid that she shouldn't be expected to screen every call like a nut, like I am doing. I told her to just say that I'm fine. Then she asked, "What if he asks where you've been? Or what you've been doing?"

I told her, "You can just say, 'Ben, Jess's fine, and I think that if she wanted you to know where she is or what she's up to, she'd call you,' and then 'OK, take care.'" Or something like that. And then I made her reenact a call from Ben to practice what she would say. She failed miserably. Eventually she got the hang of it. Our attempts went something like this:

Me: (as the phone) *Brrrring. . .brrrring. . . .*

Abigail: Hello?

Me: (as Ben) Uh, hi, Abigail, sorry to bother you again— this is Ben.

Abigail: (already too cheerful for my liking) Oh, hi, Ben! How are you doing?

Me: I'm fine, thanks. I just called to ask, did you get in touch with Jess?

Abigail: Yeah, Ben, she's fine.

Me: So do you know where she's been?

Abigail: (nonchalantly) I think she was away for part of the weekend with friends, but she's home now.

Me: (laughing and no longer in character) Abigail, why are you telling him about me? And making shit up! Look, the deal was you were gonna say I'm fine and anything else he wants to know is for me to tell him, should I choose to.

Abigail: (giggling) Oh, sorry. I forgot.

Me: OK, let's try that part again. I am Ben. So, Abigail, where's Jess been?

Abigail: (dead serious) I'm sorry, Ben, I am not at liberty to disclose that information.

Me: (laughing hysterically, as is Kim, overhearing the discussion) Oh, my God! What the fuck is wrong with you? What are you saying? Like, I got a court order or you've been sworn to secrecy. He's going to think I joined some witness protection program or I'm actually a CIA agent. "Not at liberty to divulge classified information." Why don't you just say, "I'm sorry Ben, that's top-secret information and I will self-destruct in five seconds if I tell you." Or, "Ben, if I tell you, I will have to kill you." What is so hard about saying, "Ben, Jess's fine. Anything else she wants to tell you I'm sure she will tell you herself"?

We're all cracking up by this point.

Abigail: OK, I'm sorry. Let's do it again.

Me: (as Ben) Hey, Abigail, so where's Jess been?

Abigail: Ben, I think if she wanted you to know, she'd tell you. And Ben, I really think you two should work this out on your own. I really don't want to be caught in the middle. This is something you both have to figure out with each other. I'm sorry, but I think you should leave me out of your relationship.

Me: (as me) Oh, Jesus. Why does it have to be so complicated? I mean, you're right, he shouldn't involve you, but can't you just tell him politely that it's none of his business? The less you say to him, the better. I mean, you can say you don't want to be involved, and, of course, it is your right to tell him so since his calling is kind of a violation of your privacy. But can't you please just say, "If she wants you to know more, she'll tell you." My life is none of his business. He made his bed. Let him lie in it.

Abigail: OK. Got it. Ask me again.

Me: Abigail, where has Jess been?

Abigail: Ben, that's her business. If she wanted you to know she'd call to tell you. Anyway I'm in the middle of a lot of stuff right now so take care, OK? Bye.

Me: (still cracking up) OK. That's good! Thank you. That's exactly the right answer. And it's the truth too, if I wanted to call him, I would. It's not right for him to involve you. Fuck him.

I WENT TO WORK, AND NOW I'M BACK, and something concerning is happening with this computer, which is like eight years old, because the last few sentences I wrote before leaving this morning somehow got erased. This bothers me, because I don't understand how it can happen. I also made a back-up which I keep on a disk. And that too is erased. And the same thing happened yesterday or the day before.

It's not like that much is missing, but why should any-thing be? I wonder if I'm doing something wrong when I save things or shut down the computer or something. It is also strange because both times things were erased, they were about dreams I've had.

The first thing that got erased was a brief discussion in which I described, to my mother, the dream with the animals in the elevator. She had made an interesting ob-servation about the part when Abigail, Lisa and I were going to steal something. Mom asked me, "What is steal-ing to you? What does it represent?" Then she pointed out that she views it as a symbolic attempt to fill a void when people who don't need to steal do. And I agreed that it was pretty interesting that, in the dream, I was with Lisa and Abigail because they're my two closest single friends. It's like maybe since we are all uninvolved, I see us as look-ing to fill a void that my married friends have already filled. This really made sense when I recalled what David said, which I feel is true, about how much emphasis I place on being in a relationship.

Then Mom suggested that taking in the stray cats and the puppy is like what I do in relationships. I tend to enter into them with people who seem always to have some major flaw, like they are too distant, or too dependent, or too immature, or too old, or some combination thereof. She worries, as I do sometimes, that I choose these people because I know it won't last. And that I do that because I don't really want a relationship, just the *pretense* of being involved or the occasional companionship. I am not sure if this is the case, but, again, it does concern me too. On the other hand, won't any partner be flawed? I guess what matters is the type and the extent of the flaw. Like abusive alcoholic versus sloppy workaholic: Not all flaws are created equal.

Anyway, today something else got erased. I wrote about a dream I had last night that Ben was going camping or fishing with a male friend and, for some reason, Ben's mother was visiting me, as was my mother. And I was trying to get Ben's mom to help me understand the break-up, either thinking that he's her son and she knows him, so maybe she could speculate intelligently about why he wanted to break up, or maybe, better still, he told her the actual reason and she could enlighten me. She was not very helpful. It seemed like she didn't know and wasn't terribly interested. She was not in the least unpleasant, just vague and unconcerned. Mom was just kind of there bonding with Ben's mom. They really hit it off in my dream and I think would have in real life as well. Ben's dad was a big executive in the Catskills. Ben said he grew up with Sinatra and Jerry Lewis always at his house. My mom would have had so much fun around all that Hollywood glitz and glam. One more thing to be sad about.

I have no idea what the dream means, but like all my

other thoughts and dreams, I think it would probably be obvious to someone educated and objective. However, my biggest concern is that more—in fact, all—of this work could be lost by the computer. Or by me. Maybe I am unconsciously losing things I find painful to preserve. I don't know, but I do find it strange that the malfunctions, both times, were dream-related. It's eerie, and now I'm wondering if I can't trust either myself or this old computer (is there a paranoid or superstitious stage in Kubler-Ross' mourning process?), and that I should print this out so I can't lose more of what I've already successfully saved.

That's interesting. It seems I'm having an issue with loss, feeling I can't hold onto what I value. But at least I'm not freaking out about it. I'm taking charge. I'm going to print what I've got to protect myself from further unwanted deletions. I am proud of myself, undaunted by minor supernatural or self-sabotaging setbacks. This is healthy. Now, of course, watch my printer not work. That would *really* freak me out. It would make me so uncomfortable on a multitude of levels.

The printer worked!

So the printer does work, and I'm happy about that, but the part I just wrote after getting home from work, about my data-losing problems, printed the first time and then got erased! Curious. I made two copies because my roommate from college, Gwen, is in from Boston, and I wanted to give her one. On the first copy, the last few paragraphs came out fine. But when I printed the second copy, they somehow got lost. So I just re-wrote them from the first copy. But I don't like that. Why is that happening?

# MORNING #8

TODAY IS THE 4TH OF JULY, and it's Tuesday. Neither of these things is of much importance to me, but I do feel sad that it's a holiday and I am not with Ben. Not that I particularly like holidays or fireworks or crowds, but I like Ben, so it's still sad.

It was really good to see Gwen last night. She came over around 7:30 p.m., and I showed her the apartment, which she'd seen dozens of times, but I had to point out all the little changes I'd made. And then we went to dinner nearby. At dinner, luckily we had a booth, so we had privacy as I rambled on about the break-up with Ben. At some point after he and I had broken up, I did speak a little about it to Gwen when she called to say she was in town, but at the restaurant I filled her in on all the heartbreaking details. Naturally, I started crying, but Gwen is another friend whom I'm not embarrassed to cry in front of. And if my life continues to go as it's been, this may become my top priority when choosing a friend—can I cry in front of them? If yes, OK, they pass, friend-material.

Then I begged Gwen to please tell me something, anything, bad about anyone she knew, so that I would feel less like the only miserable, rejected woman out there. And as luck, bad luck in one sense, would have it, she had a great story about her sister. The story was great for a few reasons. First, because I know Gwen's sister and she's beautiful, smart, and successful, which honestly made it far better than hearing a story about some loser getting rejected. The loser-story would be less relatable, since I still have my inflated ego in spite (or because) of my myriad insecurities.

The second reason the story was so great was that it was actually quite similar to my own.

And lastly, it was so good because it happened recently, like within the past six months, and I don't know why that's better than if it happened a long time ago, but it is.

Oh, one other reason it's good is because Eloise, Gwen's sister, is a few years older than I am, so that also made me feel better.

Anyway, Gwen's sister met this guy at work. And basically they hit it off right away and were really hot and heavy and going away every weekend together, and even took a trip to London in the first few weeks that they were dating.

I asked Gwen if Eloise thought she loved the guy, and she said she wasn't sure, but suffice it to say, they were really involved and there was all this intensity, and that's good enough for me. They don't have to say the L-word for me to know that this is something in which Eloise was becoming heavily invested. Because, you know, she has to be really invested if she's spending all her time with the guy and for her to be really hurt by its ending, and that's what I needed for the story to make me feel any better. I needed pain.

So things were great and he was getting her really thoughtful and painstakingly selected gifts, and spending lots of money, and they were inseparable. And he made mention of having this habit of pulling away from relationships when they got too intense. But he also made a point of telling her that:

1. He had never discussed this with any other woman. He said he had never cared enough about anyone to share this personality "thing" and prepare them for it.
2. He felt differently with Eloise than he had with any one else.

So she's thinking, OK, this is a wee red flag, but now we've discussed it so if he starts to freak out, which maybe he won't since he says he feels differently about me than any of those other chicks, at least I've been warned, and we will be able to work through it.

But, of course, around three months into the relationship that "thing" started to happen, and he broke up with her.

I asked Gwen if he just broke up with Eloise, or if he tried the let's-see-other-people approach (note that I've become a pro at the different ways these break-ups can go). She said she thinks he did the let's-see-other-people, but that Eloise felt about that the way I did, that it's more pain than it's worth. Plus, isn't that really just another way to say you're ending things?

Then I asked Gwen, perhaps cynically, as if I have a monopoly on sadness and self-pity, if Eloise was really, *really* upset. She was.

"Did she cry?" I asked skeptically.

"Yes, Jess, she cried." Gwen said this in her kind of patient, amused way. And I knew it had to do with something that she realized about my personality long ago. I can't put into words what it is, but I know that it's not about me being mean or reveling in other peoples pain (usually), although I know that's what it may seem she's responding to. Actually, I think it may have to do with the fact that Gwen already knows full well that I often ask obvious questions, ones to which I already know the answer, just because I like to hear the response. Like, I want to hear her say it, even though I know. She was probably amused by how predictable I am. She was also probably aware of how much of a misery-loves-company kind of girl I am.

So the Eloise story was comforting, even though I am sorry for her. Mostly, I'm sorry for me. And it was kind of good to know that they've not gotten back together because increasingly I've been feeling that Ben and I won't, so it helps me to avoid living with false hope. If they had gotten back together I might be more inclined to think that Ben and I will. But we're not them, and I think we aren't getting back together regardless of what other couples do. Moreover, it's better just to believe that this is how it's going to be than to keep waiting for something that's likely not going to happen.

Then Gwen and I came back to my place and played some Mortal Kombat, which I knew she expected to hate but which I thought she might actually really like but, to her credit, she did not. And we talked some about her, but not that much because I kind of monopolized the conversation. I did it in part because I was rambling on about Ben and in part because I knew that if we talked too much about her, I'd be really bummed because in spite of her humble, downplaying of things, by all accounts, her life is perfect.

She's getting her Ph.D. in something that really interests her (I think it's women in France during the fascist movement of the 1920s and '30s). She's been living for five years with this guy, Mike, whom she went to high school with, and to whom she, in high school, lost her virginity. They were not really dating back then or when they went to college, but they were great friends and she just loved him as a person which somehow makes it all the better. They went to separate colleges, dated other people, and realized that they're happiest together. Plus he's ridiculous. He went to Princeton undergrad, Harvard for his M.A. in Architecture. And if that's not enough, he's drop-dead gorgeous and truly doesn't know it. He's also just a sweetheart, funny, and now (what with architecture jobs being scarce) he's a drummer in an up-and-coming rock band that just got signed by a well-known record label. Oh, and he's also a gifted, self-taught chef who has worked in five-star French restaurants or something. I think she may have said she comes every time they have sex. Oh, and that they still have sex most days of the week. She could be making this up, but if she said it, I believe her. I mean, even on a good day, it's hard to hear Gwen talk about her life. Plus, she looks so fucking put-together. She's got this kind of very classic, stylish, European way of dressing. She's one of those few people who can wear a tiny scarf without seeming annoying or pretentious. That's really a feat. I usually hate those tiny-scarf wearers. They're so fake.

Gwen called me today to say "hi" and told me she read a copy of the story I gave her last night. I was pleased but not surprised. Frankly, I would've been pretty disappointed if she hadn't read it. I made copies that didn't include the fucking my landlord part since it's really embarrassing. She said that she liked it, and some of it made her laugh, but of course, she couldn't deny that she felt sorry for me and was a bit worried that all I do is take pills and smoke cigarettes. I assured her that this is not usually a way of life, but largely a response to the past week's events, which is true. Though I always smoke, I am doing so more now. And I generally go for long stretches of time without any Valium. In fact, the whole Valium thing is a very recent development. Like, it's only been for the past year or so that I've been getting it. And not until the past few months did I even try to do so with any regularity. Actually, it started when my mom moved to New Jersey. She asked me to go to our shrink (the one who yells) to get her prescriptions. I had been going once every month or so to get them for her, and one of the many things she takes is Valium.

One time I asked him, "Hey, can I get some Valium?" And he wrote me a prescription. Just like that. And that's how it started. But he doesn't always give them to me when I ask. Part of why I get them is just that I like the comfort of having them around for emergencies. And they're fun to take with friends. I end up giving a lot of them away.

Another interesting thing—before Gwen even had the chance to tell me she'd read the story, I asked her, "Did you read it?" And then, upon finding that she had, "So what did you think?" And then maybe even, but I don't remember, "Did you like it?"

What the hell is there to think or critique? It's like this started as my way of dealing with some very personal and difficult thoughts and feelings, and soon I'll be out canvassing for a publisher. What's my fucking problem? Is nothing sacred? The problem is not that I gave this to Gwen to read, and not that I have let—nay, practically *forced*—virtually everyone to whom I've spoken in the past week to listen to or read excerpts of this; it's that I'm asking for fucking *feedback*. Feedback about my life!

And part of that, I'm sure, is healthy and understandable. Like I'm asking, "Do you get anything from this that can help me better understand myself, or Ben, or what happened?" since I have no objectivity. So I'm OK with my looking to others because, as I mentioned, I feel some of what is going on may be obvious to them and just isn't to me because I am living it.

But these are my deepest thoughts about one of the most painful experiences I've had to date (no pun intended) and I am really asking, "But what do you think of the writing? Can you check it for spelling or grammar? Are there any changes you'd like to make or anything you think I should have omitted?" Am I that removed? Am I not, and this is an attempt at being so? It's like I have no real feelings. Everything is up for discussion. Nothing is too personal or my very own. But that's my doing. And what's worse, I am not eager to change it. Soon Gwen will be going back to Boston, and she mentioned (and before even saying anything, I had thought it) that it would be nice if I could keep sending her installments. And I want to. I will. So I had already considered it before she even brought it up. And then we talked about how psyched she'll be to get them when she's away in France doing research for her dissertation.

Have I totally gotten away from the point of all this furious writing? Will I *ever* really figure out what the point was?

And in my usual detached way, I find this bizarre behavior more interesting than upsetting. It's like everyone can upset me but me, whom I simply find amusing and curious and, I'll admit, much more clever than I probably should. It's as if I'm going to spend this life observing me and maybe, if there is a next life, I'll try living it—see what *that's* like. Just for a change of pace, you know.

I remember once, when I was about twenty-two or twenty-three, I had a job in social work. I don't remember if I was depressed or what exactly was going on, but I was talking to a co-worker and told him, "You know, it used to be like I wasn't living life but watching it, as one would a movie or TV show, but the weird thing is that it's like I'm not even doing that anymore." I had completely stopped participating. And I don't even think I was unhappy. In fact, I think I was kind of haughty and feeling this was not even worth my time—"this" being what? My life? Living? And as I write this, I think that this feeling must surely be a defense mechanism.

And then I worry about what is, or was, so bad in my life that I needed to adopt this detached outlook to get by. And then I think, hopefully, maybe this is just something like the Valium that I keep around, as David (dry doctor) would say, "prophylactically." Maybe there was, at some point in my childhood, as in everyone's, some pain or discomfort, and maybe it dawned on me that the less involved I was, the less pain I felt and, as is my tendency, I took that discovery to the extreme, and now I've got this wall that I never really needed and is much higher and stronger than I ever meant it to be.

But then I wonder, is this really the case? And if so, what can I do about it? And I can tell you right now that, for me anyway, there's not necessarily any correlation between realizing something about oneself and fixing or changing it. Maybe you need to know what the problem is in order to address it, but I've had the same problems for ages, been aware of them for ages, been in therapy on and off for ages, and. . .well, need I say more?

How do I open myself up to this life? This questioning is frustrating, particularly because, even as I wrote the last question about how to let myself feel, I was thinking, Isn't it maybe the case that I feel too *much* and not too *little*, and that's why I have built this wall?

I suppose that was always the assumption. Why have it, this shield, if not as a result of sensitivity? But then, just how sensitive am I? What's my fucking problem? I don't even think I'm *that* fragile, even without my wall. It's kind of a nice wall at times, but it's bad too because one can't totally avoid pain and still feel the greatest degree of pleasure. I don't know this for a fact, it's sheer conjecture, but I strongly suspect it. It does make sense.

Anyway, I don't think this is a problem that's going to get solved in one session with myself, so I'm moving on. (Oh, God, am I moving on because I am close to some sort of breakthrough and it's too heavy? Should I force myself to stay on this topic? Nah.)

Anyway, remember my dream about the cats in the elevator? Well, last night, as I was walking home with Gwen, I saw this cat by my building. I never see stray cats around the neighborhood. And I don't think I mentioned it, but that's how I got my cat, Kitty, about five years ago. I was living in Chelsea, and she was outside my brownstone for two nights in a row; it was winter, and I fed and played with her, but I didn't take her right away because a lot of the people living around there had little backyards that they let their cats run around in, so I figured she belonged to somebody. But when I discovered that she was declawed, I decided that she'd either run away or someone had put her out. And to leave a defenseless cat on the street is like the height of cruelty.

So I decided, "Fuck you, she's mine," to whomever she belonged. And I admit I didn't post any *Lost Cat* signs either, as I may have told some friends I had. There's probably a little boy named Timmy, who is now ten and still cries daily to his parents about how much he misses Sparky, his declawed tabby who mysteriously disappeared when he was five. Listen, I don't want to hear about it! She's got the best fucking home a cat could have. She and my other cat, Kat, have their own *bathroom,* for Chrissake. (Well, they don't *each* have their own bathroom; I mean they share one. But it's separate from mine. And, yes, my bathroom is bigger, but so am I.)

Anyway, there was this cat by the building last night, and I asked the doorman if he knew about it and if it was the building's cat or did it belong to someone. He said it'd been coming by for like two years, but I'm not sure I believe him because first he said ten years, and this is that doorman, Troy, who is always joking with me. So I don't know what to make of the cat appearance. I don't know if my dream is a sign that I should adopt it. Maybe my dream was a warning. Maybe this is the Cat of Doom, though I highly doubt it.

Dream or no dream, I'm not sure I want another cat. It's bad enough that I got Kat to keep Kitty company— worst thing I ever did to shy little Kitty. About two years ago, I decided that she should have a playmate for when

I'm not around. I knew that she was very timid, and she may have been abused before she came to me, but I thought she still might like a fellow feline friend.

So I adopted Kat from a rescue shelter. I picked the least threatening companion I could find. I got a male, thinking two females might have some territorial thing happening. I got a kitten, thinking that this way he would have no prior experiences with other cats, and Kitty could kind of show him the ropes. I brought him into *Kitty's* home, thinking her scent would be everywhere and he would bow to her seniority. He had one eye because of an infection at birth. I cut his balls off! And the fucking thing still bosses Kitty around. I don't know who's more annoying: Kat for doing it, Kitty for letting this unpleasant precedent to be set, or me for creating the situation. Basically, as I see it, Kat is normal and Kitty is not. He goes over to her a lot of the time with the intention of lying near her, or grooming her, and she runs away. And he thinks it's a game and gives chase. It's not really all that bad. Sometimes she even lets him clean her, or sleep in the chair with her. He means no harm, and I love him very much.

Essentially, Kitty is just like a cat, and Kat is like a dog. In some ways Kitty *is* a bit doggish, too—for example, she knows her name and almost always comes when I call.

So does Kat. But Kitty is fine as a cat. There's this thing about her—I only have to look in her direction and she's purring. I've never seen any creature so grateful for the least bit of attention, although I try to give her a lot. And the minute you say her name, her tail sticks up happily in the air. And we talk, which Kat and I do not do, or at least I talk to Kat but he doesn't talk back. Kitty and I have long conversations. They're not terribly deep. They usually go something like:

Me: (Always a bit sing-songy) I love you, Kitty.
Kitty: (Long and drawn out) Meeeeeooooooow.
Me: Kitty?
Kitty: Meow.
Me: Are you my Kitty?
Kitty: (Often it's kind of gurgling because she always purrs when we talk) Meow.
Me: Little Kitty.
Kitty: Meow.
Me: How're you doin', small Kitty?
Kitty: (Sometimes it's like a short quack) Meow.
Me: Hello, you.
Kitty: Meow.

You get the gist. Actually, that's more than just the gist, that's *it*. Those are our discussions. Maybe Kitty is really annoyed and thinking, Why can't we ever talk politics or physics?

Unlike Kitty, Kat is not a big talker. But also unlike

Kitty, Kat is not timid. He will walk freely over me and knead me with his paws. Kitty will only kind of hop nervously across me to get to the other side. And Kat reaches up, so I'll hold him! Like a baby. Kitty doesn't like being held, but I do it anyway. And maybe other cats do this but *I* have not experienced it: Kat growls when somebody's at the door. It's like low and deep, and once that person is inside, he's super affectionate, but he'll growl when they're outside. Sometimes. Not always. I haven't noticed any kind of pattern in terms of when he growls or at whom. As far as I know, it's never happened when I've been the one entering.

Also, possibly since Kitty won't usually permit him to groom her, Kat grooms me. My arms. My neck. My face (which I don't usually permit either, because it hurts). That tongue is mighty rough, and the breath's not great. But he's so fucking cute. He's what my mother would call a "mush." Just very loving. As is Kitty, but in a much daintier, kind of pathetic way. She always seems to want to let down her guard, but for some reason she can't. And even though this is sounding a bit like my wall discussion, I relate more to Kat who is very outgoing because my wall is very internal and Kitty's is very conspicuous.

Another way, I just realized, in which Kat is like a dog is that he drools when he's being affectionate. This happens a lot, and it's very cute and very disgusting. Another interesting habit he has involves his desire to sit on my lap whenever I'm on the toilet. He jumps onto my lap each and every time I'm in the bathroom. Sometimes I wonder how it came to be that my being on the toilet signifies our special time together. He tries to join other people there, too. In fact, anyone in my home can expect a whole lot of loving from Kat while going to the bathroom.

Somehow, thinking about Kitty and Kat and how much I love them, and knowing that Ben is allergic to them and that I probably would have had to consider finding them other homes if he moved in, and how sad that would be, doesn't help me feel better about the break- up. I would have ditched them for him, but I am glad that I don't have to. Actually, I'm not certain I could've parted with them. But in all likelihood, I would have. Is that awful? It is moot anyway.

It's 8:30 p.m., and I'm sleepy. I haven't eaten anything but a few pieces of grapefruit all day, since when I went out this morning to buy coffee, cigarettes, and cat food, I wasn't hungry, and I forgot to get something for later. There's no food in the house except for a few dozen ancient cans of Campbell's Condensed Cream of Mushroom Soup. It's Dad's favorite, so they stocked up on them when he and Mom lived here. I don't think it's all that "M'm m'm good!" Or all that "M'm m'm healthy!" Or "M'm m'm anything I'm even remotely in the mood to prepare or eat."

And then I didn't feel like going out again.

Plus, I'm low on cash so I don't want to order in. So I think I will tuck myself into bed to read *Time's Arrow* by Martin Amis, which I've been thoroughly enjoying, not because, but in spite, of the fact that Ben gave it to me and every time I look at the cover it reminds me of the little bastard.

# NIGHT #9

KAY, IT'S LIKE 1:00 A.M., so more like Day #10 than Night #9, and I haven't eaten a thing all day, which I'm not proud of, and had a fair amount to drink, but I'm not tired and I don't completely feel like writing though I feel I have to because I will feel guilty or unproductive or somehow unfulfilled if I don't.

It's similar to when I'm in exercise mode. I'm scared to stop. And it's hard for me because I keep making mistakes, and not minor ones that I can go back and fix, but big ones that I have to change right away or I fear it won't make any sense when I return to it tomorrow, sober and with some food in me. I don't know why I am not eating. I do want to lose weight, but this is not a smart way to do it, and I'm not *so* short of cash that I can't buy something cheap like pasta or a sandwich. There is a lot I have to say but I'll just mention a few things that I will elaborate upon tomorrow when I have more energy:

1. I worked today and have someone interested in the studio, so that's a good thing.
2. Part of why I didn't write sooner and why I am a little drunk, though not overly, is because Kim came over with her friend Mark. We shared a bottle of wine and then had coffee with Kahlúa, and that's all I've "eaten" today. They stayed late, and after they left I spoke for an hour to my friend Shelly, whom I've known since freshman orientation in college. She's really interesting. She's from Great Neck from a wealthy and conservative Jewish family. She's all tattooed, and half her head is shaved, the other half is blue. I guess you could say she's the blue sheep of the family.
3. I also want to mention, as if there's any chance I'd forget, that I spoke with Ben. He called when Liz was over today after work, before Kim got here. I didn't pick up the phone but called him back after Liz left in the short time between then and when Kim arrived. His message was just, "Jess, will you please just call me back, just once. Thank you." He wasn't really pleading, more frustrated-sounding. When I called him, I got his answering machine and left a message: "Hey. It's me. Call when you get a chance." No big deal.

I don't know why I called him back—not like I really regret it, just that I'm not sure what prompted me to this time as opposed to all the times when I didn't answer the phone or return his call. Anyway, when he called back, Kim and Mark were over, and I went into the other room and we talked for a little while. It was . . .I don't know. I kind of opened up to him. He asked me what I was doing not answering the phone and not calling him back, and I told him I wasn't sure I wanted to speak to him, and he said that I should have at least said that to him (like it wasn't obvious), and then I asked, "Ben, what the fuck happened to you? Like, why did you do this?"

And he said, "Well, officially, you were the one who ended it."

"But come on," I said. "You were telling me you wanted to see other people, and I don't think that can happen anymore. Why did you do that?"

He said, "I know that I love you and that I'll never replace you, but I have this longing to be single and to flirt with other women. . ."

"But I don't understand," I said. "I thought we talked about that. Like we each knew that we liked to flirt, and that being involved didn't mean we weren't attracted to other people, it was just that we really wanted to be together. This is probably going to sound annoying, but maybe you're not old enough to feel like I do. I can't *date* anymore. It's like, I know every person is different, but they're all the same, too. Like every date is both different and the same, and dating is just like stagnation to me."

At the time I didn't think to say it, but I feel like dating is like running on a treadmill. Like the way cartoon characters seem to be heading somewhere but the background just keeps repeating itself.

"I know—I'm crazy," he sort of sighed. "I feel the same way. But then why do you think I stopped wanting to sleep with you?"

"My pussy stank?"

"No, besides that."

"Well, I'm sure part of this is ego but I also think it makes sense. . .I think that it really had very little to do with sex and had mostly to do with your desire to withdraw and with your difficulty with intimacy. I think you decided that you wanted out, or decided that you *wanted* to want out, and the sex part followed. I mean, the sex was good, and I know I don't look any different than I did when you were into it."

"You're right. Let's get back together."

"No!" I said, laughing and not even excited or tempted by this impulsive and immature exclamation. I knew he both did and didn't mean it.

In reality, I think he was a bit drunk at the time, and I know I was a little buzzed because I purposely wanted to be before he called me back, in case it was a really bad talk, especially since I'm out of Valium.

Then he asked me if I had slept with or fooled around with anyone. I, not sure I should have, told him the truth—that I hadn't. He didn't believe me. Of course, it's only been like a week!

"Not even John?"

"No."

"You're lying. You know you fucked him."

"I didn't! Especially now that I've been tested and I'm like pure as the driven snow AIDS-wise. And I've decided that, since I don't have it, now I can avoid getting it, so I can die from something else like cancer or getting hit by a bus, but I'm not risking my life to get laid."

"Yeah. I know what you mean. It's kind of like being a virgin," he said.

"Exactly."

"I haven't been with anyone either," he volunteered.

I hadn't asked and I don't think, for some reason, I'd have been too upset if he had but, of course, I prefer that he hasn't. Unless he's lying. I don't think he has been with anyone else, and I don't know why I don't think it would have mattered much to me if he had. I suspect it's because I know with what ease he can have meaningless sex, so it wouldn't necessarily have been a threat in terms of his feelings for me. I don't think his banging some chick would in any way diminish what we have. . . had. . .

have? on an emotional level.

There was a little more, but I have to say that John called soon after I began writing about my conversation with Ben, and I am writing this while I am on the phone with him, and I'm still on the phone with him and so distracted and I can't believe he would subject himself to this kind of abuse or, at least, neglect. I'm talking to him right now but still noisily typing away at the computer. He just asked me what I'm writing and I was vague and just said "my story," because I don't want to be mean and tell him it's all about Ben.

And now I realize that he is, right at this very moment, in the process of telling me about how two of his old girl-friends, one of whom is a model, and the other who just "looks really good," both want him back. And as I was losing respect for him, thinking that this is an obvious and childish ploy to make me jealous, just now he added that meeting me illustrated to him how much he wasn't really compatible with those other women and he couldn't see himself ending up with them since he's met me. So now I feel flattered and guilty for being so cold and inattentive, and typing the whole time we've been on the phone, and for assuming the worst of him. I mean, it was his choice to stay on with me, but still. . .

"I'm sorry," I blurted out even though he had no idea what I'd been writing.

"Why?" he asked.

So I read the part about thinking badly of him and then feeling guilty and apologetic, and he laughed. "You see, you were ready to think ill of me. But I wasn't doing that at all."

# MORNING #10

'M LEAVING FOR WORK SOON, but I spoke to John last night until like 4:00 a.m., and we had a lot of fun. He was so sweet and at one point he said sort of wistfully, "Jess, I'd really like to kiss you. I remember how nice it was to kiss you." And he talked about how much he loves me and misses me and thinks there's no one as great as me. . . and I feel sorry for him because it's like he's relinquished all his power.

He seems so honest and vulnerable, and he's so demonstrative, and, in my usual way, I feel a bit suspicious. Is he being manipulative? Does he say to his friends after we talk, "Girls love that mushy shit"?

But I don't think that's him. I think he means everything he says. That's so amazing, and I'm so lucky to know someone who both feels these things for me and doesn't hesitate to say them.

But you know, it's kind of a turn-off, too, like, "You don't hear me saying these things back to you so maybe you should get a little self-respect." I don't know. He makes me feel so mean, but also so powerful, and I do think he's manipulative—but not in a malicious way, just that he knows which buttons to push, except in bed.

One thing I do know is that things are changing with regard to my feelings for Ben. I'm better. I'm not sure why. It's possible that it is because last night's discussion left me hopeful that we might get back together one day, but actually, I think it might be for just the opposite reason. When we talked, I felt so much *older* than him emotionally, and more together, and like he's a conflicted young man about whom I can easily see myself thinking of less and less as time passes.

I just got home and spoke to my mother. She's "my mother" and not "Mom" when a discussion has gone poorly. She asked me what I'm doing tonight, and I told her that Kim is coming over with Steve. And Kim's going to cook dinner.

"So. . .you're seeing a lot of Kim," Mom said critically.

"I have a date tomorrow night," I offered, hoping to appease her.

And I do. This guy I have known for the last six months or so has been pursuing me heavily. Coincidentally, I met him the same night I met Ben, at the same bar. We started chatting, and he's not that good-looking but he does have a really good personality. He's funny and quick, and I gave him my number, which I don't usually do if I'm not psyched about someone. I have this big privacy thing—my number's unlisted, and I don't readily give my last name or address to strangers. I guess that's normal, but I am acutely aware of trying not to have my space violated.

Actually, I probably just gave him my number because I was drunk when we met. And he proceeded to call me a lot. And whenever he reached me, I was nice to him and actually enjoyed talking with him, but if he ever called and I wasn't home, he'd leave a message, and I never felt like calling him back. And when he'd ask to get together—for months—I couldn't because I seemed always to have plans. And I wasn't trying to avoid him, I was just busy. I guess I could've made time for him but didn't care to.

I was kind of juggling John and Ben back then. And sometimes he'd say, "Well, I'm not going to keep doing this, so why don't you call me when you're free to get together." And I would say, in earnest, "Okay, that sounds like a good plan." And then I would never call. But he still would. And for a while he would preface every conversation with, "This is the last time I'm calling you." But it never was. And then, once, I tried blowing him off before I was seriously dating Ben and said, "Actually, I'm kind of seeing someone." But I wasn't really seeing anyone. At least not exclusively.

And he said, "Jess, we're *all* kind of seeing someone." So we continued to speak occasionally. And once he said, "I don't know why I keep calling you. It's not like I can't get dates." And even though he's not that cute, I believe him, so I don't know why either. "There's just something about you," he said.

Finally, before I started going out exclusively with Ben, and after like three or four months of this bullshit, I made a date with him. And he took me to a really nice restaurant. And I got drunk. And I fucked him!

I told my co-worker Liz about this today, laughing, because she was at my desk when he called and she heard me make a date with him. She asked who he was, so I told her the story. When she asked me if he was any good in bed, I told her that he was OK, but that he came pretty fast so I made him do it, like, two or three more times. And he must've thought I really liked it—or him—but I was just trying to make one of those times count. I slept at his place. But I was still dating John and Ben. And I lied to Ben about my night. I told him the next day that I'd had a date (we didn't keep date stories from each other or pretend we weren't doing things with other people), and that I'd slept over, but I denied having fucked the guy. It was that same evening that Ben and I decided not to see other people.

So this guy Terry (Terri?) dutifully called me the evening after we fucked, but I was out making my monogamy official and didn't call him back. And then he went away for a few days on business, and when he got back he called, and I told him I'd gotten serious with one of the guys I'd been dating. He wished me luck and happiness but he called another time after that, and I didn't return the call, and then he let some time pass, and when he called me today at work. . .well, Ben and I are broken up, so you can see how his persistence paid off, because I'm going out with him tomorrow night.

Today, from work, over the phone, I told Terry that he should know that I've been tested, and now that I know for a fact that I don't have AIDS, I'm not sleeping with anyone until things are kind of established. "Don't expect it to be a great evening," I warned him.

He replied, "Actually, maybe we shouldn't meet."

I knew he was joking but thought there also might be—no, definitely was—some truth to it. I guess it made me feel defensive or insecure, like he can only like me for sex. I don't even think that's all I have to offer, but I still feel that's all any guy would want from me. Is it because I'm not interesting or informed? I think I'm smart, but I have no interests or hobbies, and no real career to speak of. I purposely avoid being up on current events because they're scary. I don't play or watch sports. So I said, "Look, it's OK if you don't want to."

"Jess," he said, "do you have to be so crazy?"

I felt better then because, while I wouldn't have cared

that much, it would have been hurtful if he didn't want to get together after that. And the fact that I slept with him on our first date makes me wonder if he knew all along, somehow, that I was going to put out and that's why he kept calling. I told myself it's nuts to think he'd called for four straight months on the off chance he would get laid. But you never know.

So I told my mom, with whom I had just made up (remember our tension from a few paragraphs back?), that I'm seeing him tomorrow night. She doesn't know that I fucked him. She probably wouldn't care, but I didn't tell her mostly because he's not Jewish. She asked if he's nice and I said he was. She asked if he's Jewish, and I lied. And when she asked if I liked him, I said, "He makes a lot of money," both to shut her up and because I kind of think he might.

"That's nice," she said.

And I was like "whatever" and then it went:

Mom: Why don't you give him a chance?

I told her I had already had a date with him and this was no big deal.

Mom: Well, honey, I think it's better than hanging out with twenty-three-year-old little boys who can't commit. You know you're going to be twenty-eight soon, and there are fewer and fewer eligible men out there.

Me: You know, it's not like I forget how old I am when we're not on the phone and need you to remind me.

Mom: I could also remind you that I don't care who you date, but since you don't seem to be making a living, I'd like for someone besides me to support you. You know, you're old enough to pay your own bills, and you're costing me a fortune.

Then we fought more. I told her if she didn't like paying for me she should just stop, and she'd feel better, and our relationship would be a lot healthier—and I wouldn't have to hear her mouth. (Although for some reason, rude and bitchy as I can be, I would never actually *say*, "I don't want to hear your mouth.") And she said she'd like nothing better, but that she doesn't want me to lose the apartment because the maintenance isn't paid, or to know that I can't afford food. And of course, this wasn't an easy fight for me to have because I know she's right. I told her, "Look, I think you have every right to be upset because I know you've spent a great deal, not only on me, but on things that would enable me to be self-sufficient." I mean, what's college these days, $80,000? "So," I continued, "I think part of what's going on here is that I feel guilty, but I still feel that, if you're opposed to giving me money, you should stop." Then, out of frustration, she hung up on me, which she rarely does. I do it sometimes.

Kim called right after and I told her, "Mom just hung up on me."

Kim: Why?

Me: Because she's tired of supporting me, and she's right.

Kim: So what are you going to do?

Me: I don't know. Get a job.

Kim: Doing what?

Me: Anything. What difference does it make? Why aren't I earning a lot of money like everyone else seems to be?

Kim: Well, try to get a job that's not too shitty or else you'll get really depressed. What would you like to do?

Me: All I want to do is write.

Kim: How's real estate?

Me: Good for everyone else in the office.

Kim: Are you showing apartments?

Me: No. Except for my exclusives, which are few and far between. I guess I need to step up my game.

Kim: So I think you should just go back to showing apartments. Unless there's something else that you really want to do.

And I agree, because real estate can be very lucrative. I picked up the phone to call my mother to apologize for being such a disappointing leech—and simultaneously she was calling me! As I began to dial her number, there she was, already on the line! And that was nice. She'd been calling to apologize for hanging up on me. And we made up.

Now Kim is here cooking dinner, so I have to go. But first, she told me to write that she's cooking rice and beans because she thinks that I need details to make my "dramatic monologue" more interesting.

I guess now is as good a time as any to mention that Kim is a thesis away from having her master's in English Literature and that she does more than just babysit. Not that babysitting isn't essential if there's a baby. Also, I must say, how ironic would it be if, after having I finally returned his call, Ben never contacted me again? I say this because, when we spoke last night, he said, in parting, "I'll talk to you tomorrow." It's now 8:00 p.m., not too late, but you know me and my worrying.

# MORNING #11

YOU KNOW ME. And now you know Ben. He never called. Fuck him. It became obvious around 10:30 or 11:00 p.m. that he wouldn't be calling, and I don't know if he forgot or he's freaked out by the other night's discussion and fears we will be heading in a back-together direction if we speak daily.

Maybe it's something else. Maybe "I'll talk to you to-morrow," is just another form of "Have a good night," or "Talk soon." In any case, I care. . .but less with each pass-ing day. Lately, I've been trying not to beat myself up about having ever been with Ben. That's how changed my feelings are. It used to be (I know how weird it is for "used to be" to be only three or four days ago) that I thought this was my soulmate, who had dumped me. And I was simply going to have to move on, forever feeling this way about him. Clearly, I'd survive and hopefully thrive, but there was simply always going to be this person who was—in addition to I don't know how many others—right for me. But now I think maybe he's not my soulmate. Why do I think this? Is it just easier since he doesn't want to be with me? I don't know.

I do know that it's a little after 10:00 a.m. and I'm not dressed for work and am sitting at this computer. I love writing. I'm afraid that if I get over Ben completely, I will *stop* writing. I'm afraid if I get over Ben and still want to write, it may be very boring. I am worried it's *already* boring.

But even if my life is boring, I don't think my thoughts and observations are. And I don't even think my experiences and interactions are boring. *I* may be boring in that I don't know a lot of facts, like some people do, and don't have strong opinions. But that's partially because the more I know about the world, the more frightening it is. So I intentionally avoid knowing many things.

I guess I will keep writing. Also, there is of course the question of to whom will it be boring. And what difference does it make if it isn't boring to me? Who am I worried about? Who am I writing for? Friends? Family? The publisher I want to start shopping around for?

Well, while I do worry about what others think, the real fear is that it will be boring to me. And that *that's* why I'll stop. I think that's really healthy, though, because usually I worry about what others think and feel, often at the expense of my own happiness, but here I am concerned about me.

Now I have to go to work. I'm not even sure what day this is. I think it's Friday. I know I'm seeing that guy, Terry, tonight. I don't feel like seeing anyone. Interestingly though, I'd rather see Terry than John, even though I like John more. It's just so much *work* with John because, basically, he loves me and I'm not feeling the same, but since I really do care about him, I don't want to be mean and I'm constantly reminded of how disparate our feelings are for each other. So I feel obliged with him to seem more interested or invested than I really am because he asks me things like, "Do you miss me?" and "Do you find me attractive?" and "Say something nice to me," which isn't a question but is along the same lines.

Actually, I did a mean thing to John yesterday, by accident. Or not. But if I meant to be mean, it was not on a conscious level. I was just goofing around and meant it as a joke. He's studying for the bar, and one of the problems he and I had when we were dating, before I started seeing Ben exclusively, was that he never had time for me. I knew he liked me, he said it all the time. And he was finishing law school, which is time-consuming, I know, but I'd known other law students, and they didn't seem as busy. Of course, maybe I just liked him (because I did for a while), so I wanted to see him more than he could see me. He did admit to me that his last girlfriend, "the model," left him because he didn't have enough time for her. So maybe this is a problem he has.

Anyway, he told me the night before yesterday that he really wants to see me and talk on the phone, but that I should know that the bar date is approaching and he's going to be really busy and not to take it personally. He made it clear that he wants to pass the bar the first time, so he's gonna be studying his ass off, and that he'll have lots of time for me once he's taken it but that these next three weeks must be devoted entirely to preparation.

Mind you, it's not like I've been asking him to get together, but I guess he thinks that part of why I left him for Ben was because he had no time for me. He thinks this because I told him it was, but it really wasn't the reason—I just liked Ben more. But it seemed like a valid and easy excuse. I probably shouldn't have done it, because now he thinks it was our biggest problem, and that it will go away, and that all will be well when he's done with the bar. Unless my feelings for him change dramatically between now and then, he will be in for a nasty surprise.

So my mean joke was that, after all this emphasis on how much he wants to see me but can't for the next few weeks because it's imperative that he work, I left a message on his machine suggesting that we go away for the next five or ten days. *Someplace convenient and cheap*, I said in my message, *like Florida or maybe New England*.

The poor boy was so happy when he got the message that he overlooked the fact that I was saying we should do it right away, which of course he can't; all he heard, by his own choosing, was that I wanted to go on a romantic little trip with him.

He called me when I got home and said happily, "I got your message!"

"Wasn't it funny?" I asked.

He paused, kind of hurt and confused. Then I felt bad, and I realized that he didn't know it was a joke about how unavailable he is right now. I made him listen to it again, and he heard that my request was that we go at the very time that he has to be this law-memorizing recluse. Then he found it mildly amusing, but it was more like his hopes had been dashed.

I tried to make it up to him by saying that we really can try going somewhere after he's taken the bar, but by this time he was sort of embarrassed, and I thought that I mustn't toy with his feelings, although that was not what I meant to do.

It is because John is so hopeful and fragile that I would rather see Terry, who doesn't linger on my every word and try to read between the lines and who probably doesn't care about me at all? It's better than being in something unrequited regardless of who cares more, because that's nasty for both parties. And maybe, though I'm not as obsequious as John, this is why Ben doesn't want to see me—because I don't feel or feign indifference with him. And maybe it's kind of a drag for him, the way it is for me with John.

# MORNING #12

IT'S SATURDAY AFTERNOON. I didn't go to work yesterday and ended up hanging out with Kim. She babysat for Jack, who is about a year old, until 1:00 p.m.; then she came over and we hung out until a little after 4:00 p.m., when she had to pick up Emily from camp. We had fun. I heated up the leftover rice and beans she made the other night. We both had some, and that was all I ate.

Needless to say, stupid as this method is, I am losing weight, though I'm sure not as much as I would be if I were eating properly, exercising, and not drinking so much alcohol or coffee with cream. But it's OK for the time being.

I got to Terry's on time, at 8:00 p.m. He had made re-servations at some fancy restaurant, and then we were going to go to a comedy club. He'd asked me, when we spoke on the phone, if I was into the comedy club idea and

I said I was, but then I realized that Ben and I had been frequenting comedy clubs at least once or twice a week for a while, and I started to have all these doubts about it.

For example, Ben is probably away in the Hamptons for the weekend, but what if he's not? What if he's not away and he's at the same comedy club? As I mentioned, Terry isn't that cute, and I don't want Ben to see me with a guy whom even I don't find very attractive. Like, I've dated guys who my friends haven't considered good looking, but if I thought they were, it didn't matter. But if even *I* don't think he's cute, even in a quirky or offbeat way, it's a problem.

Next, forgetting about Terry, what if Ben is with a woman? That alone is bothersome, but what if she's really attractive? That's bad in and of itself, but factor unattractive-Terry into the equation, and. . .well, it started seeming like less and less of a good idea.

And then, having nothing to do with Terry or Ben, but having instead to do with my newfound eating disorder, dinner *itself* stopped seeming like a good idea, especially since I had eaten those three beans and a grain of rice with Kim. I mean, how is a girl supposed to keep her figure if she's gorging herself on over 500 calories a day, not including coffee and alcohol?

So eating was out. And as I mentioned earlier, sex was out too, since I am pure as the driven snow in terms of STDs.

Thus, by the time I got to Terry's place, all I wanted to do was drink and leave. Instead, I drank and stayed. And he was all over me. And I guess, if you tell a guy who's made all sorts of plans to go out and do things that you just wanna stay home with him and drink, he's going to get ideas. It's sort of a shame that they always think they are going to get some. But they're usually right, and he did. Not sex, though. And not oral sex either.

We were on his couch and he was like a damn octopus and, of course, I could have left but instead I asked, "Look, I just have to know, are you like this because, in spite of our discussion, you still think there's a chance you'll get laid? Or do you know you won't and you just wanna fool around anyway?"

When he said, "Well, a little of both," I respected his honesty—although it may have all been in the hope of get-ting laid and, perhaps, he *wasn't* being honest.

But then I told him that I stand firm on this sex thing and he was so persistent still, probably because I'd already slept with him, that he said, "Well, okay. What can we do? What's allowed?"

I could have left at this point too, but I instead I stayed and said, "A hand job. OK? Do you want it now?"

Annoyed, I started angrily undoing his belt. But he stopped me and asked, "Jess, do you think that men don't have feelings? How would you have felt if what'd hap-pened last time had happened to you?"

He was referring to the time that we slept together and, the next time we spoke, I was going out with Ben and told him, "Sorry, but it's suddenly really serious with this other guy and I'm not dating other people," and I thought, "What if that *had* happened to me? What if I had slept with a guy and called him afterwards and he didn't call me back, and then when I called him again, he told me that he and some girl were really in love."

And I answered, "Okay, so I don't think I would've called a second time if you didn't return the first call. And I'm not sure I would've called the first time either. But, in answer to your question, if I had, and what happened to you happened to me, I would have been very hurt."

"You see? It was very unpleasant for me. I felt used."

"Bullshit."

"No, I did, Jess. You think men can't feel used?"

I wondered what this had to do with the fact that he was all over me, and I said, "Look, I am sorry that you felt used and I wouldn't have wanted to be treated that way, but that's a totally separate issue. If you want to talk about that, we can, but what does it have to do with your trying to get laid right now? Is sleeping with you now supposed to make up for what happened last time?"

"Well, it would help." He was joking *and* serious.

I laughed but began to collect my things. "I think I should go."

"Please don't go," he said sweetly. "We don't have to

sleep together. We don't have to do anything. I'd just like you to stay."

So I STAYED, KNOWING FULL WELL that we wouldn't do nothing, but by that point I really didn't care too much. And though I did feel that I'd let myself be somewhat compromised, I have this fucked-up attitude that a hand job is like nothing whereas fucking or blowing him would've been a big deal.

Of course, this is just a way to rationalize permitting myself to be taken advantage of. Like why would I do *anything* if I don't want to? I guess I have low self-esteem. And the worst part is that, while I know intellectually that I shouldn't be intimate with anyone on any level if I don't want to, I'm still proud that I didn't sleep with him or go down on him.

Maybe it's a sad outlook to have. But I feel this way—doing either of those things would've made me feel like I wasn't being true to myself, but a hand job is only vaguely intimate and, more importantly, probably not an easy way to contract diseases. Then again, the hand job was without a condom whereas the intercourse would have been with one. So, actually, I had more contact with his semen than if I had fucked him. I could get worked up about this but I won't.

I think part of why I stayed is that I just wanted to be in bed with someone and cuddle. He's pretty good at that and he has a lot of body hair, which I like. Especially on a guy's chest. But I like it everywhere. I don't like beards or mustaches, but I like shadow and stubble. And I like when they've got hairy arms and legs. And I don't even care if it's on their back even though it's not necessary, and I suppose too much hair there could be a turn off, but not really. So, we cuddled and that was nice. And this morning as I got dressed:

Terry: Are you going to return my calls now?

Me: I think I will. Are you going to call?

Terry: I'm not sure. (He was smiling and seemed to be joking, but I couldn't tell for certain.)

Me: You see, I think you're joking, but the mere fact that there's any doubt that you are is the other reason, besides being pure as the driven snow, why I am so not into sleeping with people I don't know well. Like, if we had fucked last night and you said this, and I was not sure you were kidding, I'd feel really bad now, but instead I just feel right for not having done more.

Terry: Jess, I was joking.

But I don't really care that much. For the time being, I'm back in "objectively curious" mode. I am interested to see if he'll call after last night, but not much more concerned than that. It's similar to how I'd feel if a friend had gone on a date with him and told me the story.

Actually, I think he's a nice guy, and smart, and that he will call, but I don't know if I should see him again if he does. . .but I guess I don't have to worry about that now.

I just had this bad feeling that there's probably all sorts of stuff happening that I'm not aware of. I mean things I'm doing and having done to me. Like, was last night more damaging than I realize? Was it *at all* damaging? Was that date rape? What is date rape? Does it have to involve sex? Is this guy actually a manipulative dick? Am I?

Would someone reading this think, "God, how can she not see it? Has she no self-worth or awareness?" Did I let him take advantage of me just for a little human contact? Did I orchestrate the whole thing? We could have gone out. I believe he did intend to take me out. Even if he didn't really, I could've said, "Let's go get food" or "Let's see a movie or some comedy tonight." I don't think I can feel *that* used, if at all. And if some injustice was done to me, as usual, wasn't it mostly by me that it was done? And does he actually feel I *used* him? Or was that just more talk?

BEFORE I CAME HOME, I DID a little grocery shopping. I decided that, even if I'm not hungry, I should eat. So I bought some eggs and tomatoes and some fat-free cheese and made an egg-white omelet. I used three eggs, two pieces of cheese, and two tomatoes. It didn't taste great, but I think it was healthy both because of its ingredients and because I ate at all. I also bought a box of Product 19, the "fat-free multivitamin and mineral supplement cereal," and some skim milk. Maybe that will be dinner. Or maybe I've eaten enough. I'm nuts. Aren't I too old for anorexia? I know that, age-wise, I'm out of the high-risk group for schizophrenia and certain other illnesses.

Here some of the bad things about my life right now:

1. Ben broke up with me. I don't know why, but I do think that regardless of whether or not he's my "soulmate," we got along really well and I'll have trouble finding someone like him. And I miss him.

2. That Learning Annex proposal I mailed elicited no response. I am confident it was well written, and Ben and I were together when I sent it, so I was in a better frame of mind—and Kim even helped me with it. I guess I may still hear from the guy. I would, at least, appreciate the courtesy of a formal rejection if he doesn't like the idea. Here I am again, just waiting for a response and explanation. More rejection and confusion.

3. My studio deal seems to have fallen through, so I'll need to keep showing the place.

4. I'm short of cash right now, and my parents are understandably displeased.

5. I should be working, but I'm not—although that will have to stop, because this is really ridiculous

and self-indulgent.  I was making good money in real estate when I was making an effort.  At one point I was the top producer in my office.  Even when I wasn't, the money was good.

Then there are the little bad things, like I still have that varicose vein on my leg, and I now have a pimple on my cheek that's big and isn't going away quick enough.  At twenty-seven, I still gets zits.

I'm bored and lonely.  No one will ever love me, and if they do, I won't love them, and if they do and I do, they still won't want to marry me.

These should probably be up in the "major bad things" category.

Some good things:

1. I can work and make money if I put my mind to it.
2. *Absolutely Fabulous* is on.  It's a rerun.  But it's still great.
3. I have friends and family who love me.
4. I'm not old.
5. I'm not hideous.
6. I'm not stupid.
7. I don't have AIDS.

This is depressing.  Even the good things are bumming me out.  One nice thing, Abigail just called.  We spoke earlier today and she like *begged* me to go out to Fire Island with her for the day. I told her I have no money and little desire to do anything that involves leaving the house. But she said, "Come on, it'll be fun. It's cheap. I'll pay for you."

But I don't feel like doing anything major, and I didn't want her to have to pay. So when we last spoke she was going alone. But she just called and said that she fell asleep right after we got off the phone and missed the ferry or some shit, so we're hanging out tonight. I'm really psyched.

Abigail is a lot of fun. She's depressed in a really amusing, self-deprecating way, and so am I when I'm with her. She's single, too. I've known her since seventh grade, when she came to my school. We graduated from high school together and have stayed in touch ever since. She is one of my oldest friends. Lisa is my oldest friend because I met her in fifth grade. They're both great. I'm lucky.

Abigail is zany. She's always having some sort of problem that becomes like an adventure. Crazy things happen to her and I think, Only Abigail could get into this sort of bind. She's like Lucy. Actually, people have said the same thing about me, like, "Only Jess," this or that. But I'm never aware of being quirky until someone points it out to me, since it's my life and I'm just living it, and there is that lack-of-objectivity thing.

# MORNING #13

A CTUALLY, IT'S SUNDAY *AFTERNOON*. I wanted to work today but I woke up at 10:00 a.m. even though I set the alarm for 7:30 a.m. I intended to go to the office to get organized, since I wanna start working regularly again. But when I got up late, I decided to make this my last day of inactivity.

Last night was kind of a drag. Abigail wanted to go out and I sort of did too, but I didn't get my shit together until like 11:00 p.m., and by then I didn't feel like going anywhere, particularly since the plan, for both of us, was to meet men. I always find the prospect of trying to meet people such a dismal one. I hate feeling like just another generic single woman out there looking to hook up with the last eligible guy. And it always feels like all the single women out there are secretaries. It's strange, too, that I should feel this way, since I've spoken with many of them and the vast majority seem, in fact, to be lawyers. But that's nonsense. Of course, they all have different jobs, but *en masse* it feels like I'm part of a herd of receptionists even though I'm not one.

Anyway, we stayed home, and I could tell that Abigail was disappointed but I just didn't feel like going out. Part of the evening consisted of vacillating back and forth about whether or not we should meet this guy, Joel, who's been like a "phone friend" of mine for about two or three months. I've never met him and don't intend to.

It's kind of a weird, embarrassing story. About two and a half months ago, Abigail was reading through the personal section of some local paper, came across his ad, and called to read it to me because she thought he sounded like my type. It was a strange ad, something like, *Lazy woman wanted to hang out, go to clubs, sleep late, etc. Smokers, drinkers, OK.* I actually never saw the ad, but that's what I remember her reading to me.

So, being a lazy, smoking, drinking, woman, my curiosity was piqued, and I called. His message was basically the same as his ad, but now there was a normal-enough voice accompanying the text. I left my number, and he called. When we spoke, he said his name was Joel, and that he's thirty-two and Jewish, and that he doesn't have to work because he inherited a lot of money. I don't know what he considers "a lot." He said he likes to go to clubs in the city and small islands for vacations.

As we spoke, two things became apparent. First, not for any specific reason, I decided that he was lying. Second, even if he was telling the truth, he's an ass. I just don't think he's very bright. And he's not a nice person. And he's not particularly interesting. And I doubt he's attractive. Probably, he's a hideous homeless person or he has his own phone line in some asylum. So I decided not to meet him, and he didn't pressure me to. I don't vividly recall our early conversations, and he might not even have asked to meet me. But we still chatted occasionally.

Anyway, it was shortly after we first spoke that I began going out with Ben, and Joel began seeing this woman, Melanie, who is nineteen and "dresses like he likes." I told him that I'd started dating Ben, thinking he'd stop calling, and threw away his number. But he kept calling and never commented about the fact that I never called him back.

I never told him my last name, or where I live, or where I work, or anything really. I'm not quite afraid of him, but the whole situation does give me the creeps. I could tell him not to call anymore, but he calls less and less, and it's easy enough to just say, "Oh, sorry, this is a bad time," and hang up on him when he calls, as I've been doing. He's totally undaunted when I do that. He just waits a little while and calls back. I think he's probably just lonely, but I would just as soon not antagonize him. He told me that he rented an apartment in the city for

Melanie, but that he keeps the one he has somewhere in Queens. He always says that Melanie is in the other room sleeping when he calls me. I'm not sure there *is* a Melanie. I never told him that Ben and I broke up. He never tried to have phone sex with me or was vulgar or even pried much into my life.

Minus the fact that he calls my home, he's not at all invasive. He just likes to chat. He told me his last name once, but I forgot it.

None of my friends, besides Abigail and Kim, knows about him. I'm afraid to tell people because I think they'll worry about my safety. Or my sanity. Or both. I don't know why I'm not afraid of him. It occurred to me that there are probably ways for him to find out more about me in this high-tech age. Maybe they sell things, like those kits and devices in the back of a rifle magazines, that could lead him to me. Do you know those ads that say shit like, *Wanna be a spy?* or *Learn all there is to know about your friends and enemies* or *Mail bombs and you?* When I think about this, I am uncomfortable. But mostly I think he's a harmless loser. Oh, God, he's definitely going to kill me.

Anyway, once when I was on the phone with him, Abigail showed up, and I whispered to her, "Guess who I am talking to? The guy whose ad you read to me!" And then I told him, because I wasn't sure it had come up before, that I actually never saw the ad, but that it was Abigail who told me about it. I asked her if she wanted to talk to him; she made a face and gestured that she didn't, but I handed her the phone anyway because I was tired of talking to him. And I was curious to see what she would think of him even though I had already formulated the opinion that I wasn't at all interested in the guy. I think I was probably dating Ben by then anyway. And I never mentioned it to Ben because it was such a ridiculous and embarrassing story.

Then I went to take a quick shower and Abigail stayed on the phone with him for half an hour. They actually hit it off a bit. But mostly he liked Abigail because he thought she seemed "bitchy," and he said he likes that in a woman. I think he may be looking for a mistress, or dominatrix, or something. He may have some role-playing stuff in mind, but we never really discussed it. It's just a sense I get. Once he said something about enjoying watching his housekeeper scrub the floor. At the time, I found it alarming, because I felt certain he didn't have a housekeeper and thought he was just lying to impress me. Upon further reflection, there may have been more to read into his statement. And as soon as I put Abigail on with him, I regretted it—not because I liked him, but because I had given him no information about me and I worried that Abigail would slip and tell him stuff like where I live, or where she lives, or where we went to school, or anything. My fear was both that she might just volunteer stuff or that she might not know which questions not to answer.

So I quickly jotted a note telling her something like, *He doesn't know anything about me, and I want it that way! Please don't tell him things about yourself either. I don't know this guy.* And she nodded that she understood, but I worried anyway because Abigail might be the person I least trust with information. She's just the kind of person who'd fuck up, like reveal your secret to someone, and then exacerbate it by immediately apologizing and begging your forgiveness—all in the presence of the person to whom she just revealed whatever it was you didn't want them to know.

Once—I don't even remember the circumstances or why it was the case, but before Ben and I were seriously dating—I had gone to some party and I didn't want him to know about it. Maybe I had gone with John and was simply trying to spare Ben's feelings. Anyway, the next night I was out with Ben and Abigail joined us and she brought up the party! I had made it perfectly clear to her that, for whatever reason, I didn't want Ben to know I'd been to this party and so she should please *not* bring it up. She brought it up. There were no harmful repercussions, but it's the principle of the thing. And I think I'm so good at *not* putting other people in compromising positions. I mean, I pride myself on generally knowing what to say, or not say, in social settings. And I guess there are people who just aren't this way, but it makes me wonder what's going on with them on some unconscious level? Are they angry? Jealous? Because telling friends' secrets is like a form of sabotage. It chips away at the very foundation that you've struggled, with your lies or omissions, to erect. It's annoying at best, and I can't help but question the extent to which anything is ever truly an accident.

Anyway, last night Joel called when Abigail was over. He asked to talk to her again, and I let him. They started talking about the possibility of all three of us getting together. Joel just wanted an opportunity to meet Abigail, and she wanted to meet him too but didn't wanna do it without me. Anyway, I wasn't going to meet him ever, and she wouldn't go alone. And we kept having him call back while we conferred. She had some feeble, irrational argument like, "Come on, he's probably disgusting, and you should find out."

"Ab [Abigail's nickname], if he's disgusting, I don't want to know. He has my number. He calls here! And if he's cute, I don't want to know. And most importantly, I don't want him to know if *I'm* disgusting or cute. I don't want him to know any more about me than he already does."

We never met him because I wouldn't, in spite of my curiosity. And we ended up telling him that my boyfriend was coming over and we were going out with him. It was a good excuse. I didn't want to tell him we'd just chickened out, because I don't want him angry with me, since he has my phone number and he's so weird. And I especially don't want to now that I've thrown his number away.

The whole point of the story is just that this is how I spent a good portion of last night. It was kind of pathetic.

And then Abigail found—and I know I generally think there are no accidents but when it happens to me there are—my printout of this story, and she started to read it. She was kind of drunk by then, and she started crying! She choked out something like, "God, why does it have to be so painful?" and "We have to be so strong" and "It's just so sad." And there was also a "Men are such scum" in there, too.

I knew she was drunk, and that she has her own baggage that she projected onto the writer—in this case, me. And that only moments before she began reading it, she'd already been on the verge of tears because her brother, Shaun, whom she idolizes, is busy with a new relationship and starting a business and has been blowing her off lately. And I just felt that it all had very little to do with my story. I *hoped* her crying did not have to do with my story, because if it was about the story, either she was upset by some disparaging remarks I had made about her being superficial or out of touch, or she was crying because she felt sorry for me, like my life is that tragic. Neither option was especially appealing. I didn't want her crying because her feelings were hurt, and even more I didn't want her crying because *my* feelings were hurt, because I've been doing such a good job of transferring all my pain onto this keyboard and not otherwise dealing with it.

Her reaction reminded me that this actually is sad, and it's all about me. It brought me back to a reality that I haven't dealt with in some time, if at all. At the same time, I was a little happy to see her crying because, since she seemed so oblivious to the negative comments I'd made about her (probably didn't understand them), I deduced, first, that she wasn't crying because she felt insulted, and, second, that maybe this writing is compelling to someone other than me.

I've got to go to sleep now, but tomorrow I'll write about having seen Dr. David tonight. And one last thing—for the last half hour or so, while I've been typing, I've also been on the phone with John, and admitting to him, as I write, because he's asking me, that I am no longer attracted to him. Or at least, I'm less attracted to him. I'm attributing it, also for his benefit, since he requests an explanation, to our lousy sex life. He says he wants to make it up to me. What's wrong with him? What's wrong with me?

# EVENING #14

'M HOME FROM WORK. It's about 6:15 p.m. I didn't have time to write this morning because I had to go to work early. Today is, officially, my first day back pounding the pavement. I didn't, though, do any of that today; instead I organized my files in preparation for showing apartments. I didn't work as hard as I could have, but it's a start.

Yesterday, David got here around 6:30 p.m. (You remember, my dry doctor. The one with whom I was unable to break up, even though it was so bad). A couple of days ago, he left a message on my machine saying that he'd figured out what was wrong with our relationship and really wanted to share it with me. He said that he thought it could help us to better understand ourselves and strengthen our friendship. I was really interested to hear what he had to say because it seemed like he'd had a major insight. I called him back and asked him to tell me over the phone what he had realized, but he said he wanted to do it in person. I don't think this was a ploy to meet with me. Anyway, we made plans to get together last night.

His realization was hardly earth-shaking. He said some stuff about noticing that I'd been pretty much angry with him from the moment we started going out, and that even though we'd both been unhappy, we must each have been getting something from the relationship since we stayed in it. He thought that what I got was someone to be mad at, and what he got was me—someone to chastise him. I agreed that we were each gratified on some level or else we wouldn't have kept at it. I mean, I don't believe that people generally stay in things without getting something from them, even when that something is a bad thing. It's like he says: I was angry a lot, but for some reason, I *wanted* to be angry then. And though I hurt his feelings a lot, for some reason he wanted someone to hurt them. When he pointed out that I was very critical of him, I jokingly responded, "Hey, I aim to please. You can't say I never took your needs into account." We both laughed.

I, of course, have thought a lot about why I was with him on and off for about three years, none of which was especially good. I think I saw being with David, brilliant Jewish doctor that he was, as a way of pleasing and getting the approval of my parents. Except that our personalities were so different, his and mine. We were hardly compatible. I think I felt it more than he did. And I was angry because, though I wanted my parents' approval, I felt like being with him was a compromise of my own happiness. Like I was doing it for them, but begrudgingly, and I was pissed. And I took it out on him as I basked in their approval. Naturally, they didn't *force* me to be with him, but I felt this was what I was supposed to do, what I had been raised to want. And I guess a good version of him, one I got along with, I would actually have wanted.

But David and I were just so different. I never felt myself, or real, with him because it never felt like *he* was real. It felt like being with someone from outer space who'd come to Earth, donned a dry doctor body, and proceeded to act the way he thought a brilliant scientist would act. I guess, in retrospect, he nailed it. And it was one of those weird things where the sex was so awkward and impersonal but his dick was so perfect, such a nice fit, that I loved it even though I'm not sure we ever even opened our eyes or kissed. Maybe that was part of why it was good.

I wonder if I could really have given anyone my parents approved of a fair chance. I think that's why I kept trying to make it work, because I worried that I was, in a way, prejudiced against him from the start because he was, on paper anyway, so perfect. And I think I thought, at the time, *Well, we, my parents and I, can't both like the same guy for me, so if they approve, he's automatically not the one.* I felt like a martyr. Then, I also wonder if I wasn't with him because it was one of those relationships that was doomed to fail, but that, for a time, had all the trappings of stability and success. And I wanted it to *look* like I had a relationship but I didn't really want one, so this was good because I knew our time together would be finite. I could appear to the world as if I were in a committed relationship but didn't really want one, and our unhappiness was forever lurking, comfortably and conveniently. It was my eventual way out, our obvious incompatibility my trapdoor, the one no one could blame me for using.

So I don't know why we were together, and therapy has brought me no closer to an answer. Maybe it's exactly what I just wrote. Maybe I didn't want a relationship. Maybe I did but never gave him a chance because I figured, *If my parents like him, I can't possibly, and I'm only doing it to placate them.*

Now it's 8:20 p.m., and Abigail is coming over, and this time I am going to get dressed and make sure we go out because it's too depressing to just sit home and talk about how miserable and lonely we are. This way, we can discuss it while we're out, in the company of strangers. *Absolutely Fabulous* is on, and I am writing this during the commercial. It's only since I've begun writing that I'm grateful for five- or ten-minute-long commercial breaks. They used to be such a nuisance. Now I run to my computer instead of the refrigerator. (I doubt that it's for people like me that they allot such an abundance of time and money to advertising.)

Terry called. Actually, I'm on the phone with him now. We're just bullshitting about nothing. He can't hear that I'm typing because he has his stereo on really loud. I feel somehow empowered by doing this secretive and private thing that he doesn't know is happening. I was going to say that it's probably how those guys who masturbate on the subway feel, but that's very different because I think they actually want people to know, and what's exciting for me is that Terry doesn't. Now he's talking about being careful about what he eats. He can only eat so many turkey burgers, and he has a really fast metabolism. Out in the Hamptons, it's hard for him to eat healthy because they're always barbecuing. Chicken has to be marinated or else it's kind of flavorless, he points out.

Abigail just left. It's about 11:30 p.m. I never got dressed. We never went out. She brought over two slices of pizza, and I vowed not to eat mine and then I did, and we watched *When Harry Met Sally* and talked about how depressing everything is. Just as an aside, I realized at some point that the story about Joel, the phone guy, is a perfect one of those "Only Abigail" or "Only Jess" stories, and the best part is that this one includes both of us. Anyway, in the movie, there was a scene where Sally's upset because her ex is getting married. And she's crying that this girl he's marrying was supposed to have been his "transitional relationship" because they had just met and it was so soon after his break up with Sally. And I said to

Abigail that I feel like everyone I've ever dated has been my transitional relationship. When will I have the permanent one?

On a whim, I called some guy's personal ad in *New York Magazine* today. He's thirty-one, Jewish, and a surgeon. I know it's stupid because I doubt anything good will come of it. First, it's a personal ad, and they don't seem like a great way to meet people. Second, he's a doctor, and I don't think I'm compatible with doctors in general, not just David. I feel like they're all bland, except the ones I go to for check-ups. They're always cheerful and full of life, probably because I'm paying them and I'm not in a relationship with them.

Anyway, he called me back, this personal-ad man, and we have a plan to meet on Thursday for a drink. I don't care about him because he's not Ben, and he doesn't sound too great outside of that. It's just something to do. We'll see what happens. Surely, I've already begun to jinx it.

I am on the phone with John now, and he's asking me why we didn't experiment more sexually—like different positions or places, and I don't know what else. I am now in the process of telling him, "John, it's because I am fat and self-conscious about allowing you a full view of my flabby white ass, OK?"

Now we're both laughing and I'm still typing our discussion, and John just said, "This story of yours, it's like really beginning to suck. It's like not even a book anymore. It's just a minute-by-minute, detailed diary of your boring life." And now we're laughing more! And I'm still typing and hearing it, he just yelled, "*See?* You are so fuck-ing *insane.* Stop *typing!*" And I'm tired and laughing too much, so I will.

# MORNING #15

OK, I'M LATE FOR WORK, and that's really bad because I have to get back into the habit of keeping normal business hours. But yesterday I noticed that it was Day 14, and that means it's two weeks since I was last going out with Ben. It seems like much more time has elapsed. And you'll notice he hasn't called me since I returned his call. We've had no contact, and I have decided to forget about my things, the stuff I left at his apartment, because to call him or write to ask for them again feels like too much of a ploy to talk to him. And I know this because I can't even remember which clothes I left there, so I must not miss them all that much. It would just be an excuse to talk to him and I think it would be embarrassingly obvious to both of us. And then, if it's not obvious to him, he's going to think that I am like obsessed with some cheap skirt or ratty T-shirt I left there, and that, too, is embarrassing.

But I do wonder why Ben won't return my things. I'd like to think it's his symbolic way of keeping something of mine, but in all likelihood he's too lazy or forgot they were even there. Probably, he threw them out. This morning I was thinking how upsetting it would be if, months from now, I received all my stuff in the mail. That would really suck because I would automatically assume that he started dating someone who was saying, "Get rid of this crap," or that for some other reason he was done needing or enjoying having my stuff in his possession, and that too would be sad. I think that I might want them back for closure and also as a way of controlling the situation. Like if he sends them back at his leisure, he's saying, "OK, I'm ready to have you completely out of my life now," like he's kicking me out. Whereas if I ask for them back, then it's like I'm saying, "I am leaving," and that's the more desirable position to be in.

I still don't know which is more upsetting, the fact that Ben is not with me or the fact that he doesn't want to be with me. Both suck. I miss him. And now I have to fucking go to work and be this independent, self-sufficient person that I know I should enjoy being, but I just don't. Ben has enough money. I thought that we were just gonna play hooky together for the rest of our lives. Maybe he knew I wanted that and it scared him. But I have some money too, so it's not like he was my meal ticket. I just thought we had the kindred, free-spirit thing going on. And I wouldn't mind my working and his working if we came home to each other. But then, increasingly, I wonder how much of this, if any, has to do with Ben. But that's part of my problem because maybe it all does and I'm just too out of touch with my own feelings to even know what's motivating them. I can't even identify them, let alone trace their origin. I don't know if this feeling I have right now is sadness or boredom. . .or maybe even joy.

Now I'm home from work. I haven't eaten a thing today besides two fat-free cookies and a half a piece of pita bread when I stopped by Kim's this afternoon. I told everyone at the office that I was going to meet a client. Then, after "work," I went to the All State with Amy, and we shared a pitcher of sangria but couldn't finish it, and I'm pretty buzzed right now since I've eaten almost nothing. I don't know why I'm not eating. It's not the money, because if worse came to worst I could ask my parents for help. And I do have some of my own money. I feel like my not eating is some sort of protest, like a hunger strike, but I don't know what my cause is. I do want to be thinner, but this is obviously some other, very unrelated, issue. I mean, I'm practically fasting, and that's not even my idea of a diet. Plus, I'm drinking so much alcohol that I'm not even losing weight.

Today I noticed that I've become rather guarded about, and even protective of, my story. But only with certain people. I'd like to say that the people who don't know me well, and who are not my close friends, are the ones with whom I've stopped discussing it, but it's really not the case. The people I don't want reading my story are those I don't think will, for whatever reason, understand it or where I'm coming from. I've been daydreaming about having it published, and then everyone will have access to it, but that doesn't matter because in that case it will be largely anonymous since most people don't know who I am.

Today, I was sitting on the back stairs of my office, smoking a cigarette with Amy, whom I still permit to read this. I've gotten into the habit of bringing a copy with me everywhere I go because I think I should look it over before I seriously consider submitting it to anybody. (I never seem to go back and read what I've written though, probably because it's too painful and also because I think I might feel compelled to make changes, and I don't want to revise it too much, as that would change it somehow in a way I don't want. I want it to accurately reflect the me then and the me now, and now-me shouldn't be messing with then-me).

Anyway, Amy went inside to take a phone call, and Liz came out and sat with me on the steps. She asked if she could read it (she already knew what it was from back when I was talking about it more freely), and I said, hesitantly, "I guess, but actually, I'm trying not to share with anyone until it's finished." I don't know why I let her read it. I think it's my problem with refusing people, like I'm afraid they won't like me or something. I'm glad she didn't ask for a handjob.

So I reluctantly handed what's become my baby over to her, and I was already uncomfortable at the prospect of sharing my innermost thoughts with this seemingly non-introspective, Jappy girl, but then it came to my attention, and she ultimately even commented, that she was just scanning it. *What? Why?* Looking for the *juicy* parts? I mean, this is my life and I'm sitting right across from you, and you asked to read it, so at least have the decency to seem interested!

I was so put off, I thought, No more stupid bitches get to read this until all the names are changed and they're giving me money to do so.

Of course, on the other hand, I was a little relieved; I hadn't wanted her to read it in the first place, so I was happy that she was not giving it her full attention. But it was still unpleasant since lately I have very little to do with Liz, and I'm discussing it less and less. I just don't want people in my shit.

Also, I realize, the more friends I badmouth, the fewer people there will be to proofread it. But I don't think that's bad. I'd rather speak my mind than censor myself and compromise to spare people's feelings. It would change the whole nature of this catharsis to try to make it a happy story that all of my friends would enjoy reading. This is so not that.

One thing that turned me off to Liz—besides the fact that she's a smug JAP lawyer one year younger than I am and married to another smug JAP lawyer, and I am jealous as all hell—is that we were sitting on the steps smoking a few days ago with this wonderful woman, Olga, who is another agent in the office, and the discussion started to leave me feeling, like, zero connection with Liz. Olga is forty-six years old. She's from Russia. For some reason, she looks like a very elegant and well put together seventy-year-old. She's been married for around twenty-five years to the same man, and she's got two grown daughters. Olga is very funny and very cynical, and hanging out with her is like reading some Chekhov play.

So Olga began telling us about an affair that she'd had with a man that lasted for three years. Her husband, to the best of her knowledge, never found out. She said that she married her husband when she was very young, and that she loves him but was never *in love* with him, and that she really fell for this other guy. She never considered leaving her husband for him, she just saw him every day or so, and loved him passionately and they had great sex.

What bothered me was Liz's reaction. Granted, Liz has only been married for six months, and she's twenty-six, so still young, but she was like horrified and amazed. "*No! Get out of here!*" she practically yelled at Olga.

"Yah, eet's true. I did it," Olga said defiantly and somewhat amused.

"No way! You're joking," Liz said, eyes and mouth gaping wide in disbelief. "How could you look your husband in the face after sleeping with another man?"

"I look him in ze face fine. I never look him so vell in the face," Olga said with that great Russian accent. "And he look me too in ze face. Vee never had such a good sex as after zat."

"I could never do that to Rob, and he would never do that to me."

"Don't be so sure," Olga teased. "Vait till you've been for twelve years married. Zat is ven I had my affair."

"Never!" Liz was obviously perturbed.

"Vhy? Vhat is so wrong? I was in love. Zay vere the best three years of my life. Everybody does eet. All men have zee affair. Vhy shouldn't I have eet also?"

Maybe Olga should have understood that a twenty-six-year-old newlywed, not from Russia and not married to the first man she ever dated, would not share this hardened outlook.

And admittedly, Olga did sort of taunt Liz about it and almost made it seem like an inevitability, which it doesn't have to be. But more importantly, it annoyed me that Liz was *so* shocked. Like it was news to her that people have affairs. Lots of people do. And of course, it's not a happy thought. And it's certainly nothing she can, or should, prepare herself for now, six months into her marriage. But her absolute horror and distain were such a turn-off. I was thinking, "Yeah, it's sad that Olga is not thrilled with her husband. But she's doing fine. More power to her. She had a blast." I totally could not relate to Liz. Why didn't she just laugh and say something like, "Well, I guess I'll hang onto my gym membership," or something. There was just no humor on her part. She was only threatened by the story, like she clearly fears it. And well she *should*, because it's people like her who that shit happens to.

And it's people *not* like her, too.

# MORNING #16

SAW JOHN LAST NIGHT. He dropped by from school, where he had been studying for the bar. We are over, he and I. I only like him as a friend now. It's actually weird to think I ever slept with him. He's so nice, but it's gone. And he's still so in love with me, it makes me sad.

I also spoke to Mom, who pointed out that either Ben must not really have cared or he's just a "shallow, fickle, young man." I think he did care, and it hurts to think of him this other way, but I think she's right. That is, I think this shallow, fickle young man did care. I called him last night and left a message on his machine asking him to return my clothes. Now it will be really rude if he doesn't, since I also sent that letter. The message I left was just, *Hi, I would really appreciate if you would mail or drop off my stuff, especially the clothes and contact lenses. You don't have to call, I'd just like my things back. Thanks.*

I tried not to sound angry or nervous but really, what difference does it make?

And Mom said, "Look, at the risk of making you angry, I think we can safely say that Ben is not coming back." This was in the same discussion that she said the thing about him never caring or just being a child. Her point was that I should just get over it.

"Yeah, you're right." It hurt to have her say it, but it was the truth.

And now I wonder if obsessing about Ben isn't just another handy means of avoiding being in a relationship. Like with David, I was in one but unhappy, so I couldn't really have been *expected* to move on at that point. I mean, I had a relationship, albeit a shitty one. And now, with Ben, I am not in a relationship but I'm depressed, so I can't really be expected to meet anyone at the moment while I conveniently grieve. I don't know. I think that our relationship meant much more to me than it did to him. He's just a kid in many ways, and it's ridiculous for me to give it this much attention. He doesn't deserve it. A couple of fun months together don't warrant this kind of mourning. I do miss how funny and sarcastic he was. But fuck it.

One unpleasant thought—the times *I've* ended relationships abruptly and very cleanly, something had happened. Often, it wasn't anything concrete or tangible, not necessarily something I could pinpoint, but I would just find myself totally repulsed by that person. Suddenly. It's happened to me a couple of times, I just shuddered at the thought of spending even one more second with some guy, for whatever reason, and I would immediately cut him out of my life. And after, I had no second thoughts. No regrets. Just relief.

So lately, I've been wondering if Ben didn't just decide that I made him sick. Like almost *physically*—if it's anything like the feelings I've had for these people from whom I was suddenly and violently turned off. I really don't like the thought of him wondering how he could ever have been with me in the first place. Or the thought of him thinking I'm disgusting. But what the hell. It really doesn't matter how he's feeling about me now, does it? I mean, if we are apart, it's no longer my concern. Or at least it shouldn't be.

I have to go to work. But I dreamed last night that this guy Tom, who is weird and worked in my office for a while, had to share my bed. And someone else, some guy I was seeing, was there too. And I didn't want Tom there, but my apartment had somehow become the only available room in some hotel. In the dream, I knew that I could refuse to let Tom stay but didn't feel like making a big deal about it. And it was a bad feeling having him there because I found him gross. And at some point, I realized that some of my things were missing and I had this hole in my temple with some kind of an external metal button and like a cylindrical sponge or gauze plugging it up. It was as if someone, I assumed Tom, had operated on my brain, and I had this open wound and access to the brain if I pulled out the moist sponge. I was concerned but not overly so. Then I was walking on the street, not *in* but toward an unfamiliar neighborhood that I knew wasn't good, and I was with some guy, and I made us turn back because it was scary.

I AM HOME FROM WORK. It was unproductive and annoying except for the three hours I spent hanging out with Kim at her apartment which is dangerously close to my office—those hours being not annoying, just unproductive. Everything else is annoying. However, for some reason, leaving Kim's today around four o'clock to go back to the office, I had a strangely gleeful moment, for no reason that I can figure. I was walking down the street, and I just felt really happy. It was a new-lease-on-life kind of feeling. Then it went away.

I'll have to ask David, but I feel like that thing in my head in my dream is called a "shunt." By the way, I'm back in touch with David. I mean, I've been in touch with him off and on since I met him like five or six years ago. But lately, we've been going through one of our speaking regularly—like every couple of days or so—phases.

# EVENING #17

OK, I'M HOME FROM WORK, and I put in a long day; I didn't rent anything, but it was productive because I made some contacts and have some leads.

Last night, Abigail dropped by with her friend Lauren. They called from the street and asked if I wanted to meet them somewhere for a drink, or if I'd like them to come by with some wine. I had been looking forward to an evening of writing and hanging out alone. Naturally, I invited them over anyway. It was fine, but it kind of sucked too, because I wasn't into entertaining and I was in a kind of sullen mood. I'm sure I didn't make a great impression on Lauren.

But then it got even worse because that guy Jonathan, the surgeon from the *New York Magazine* personal ad, called and asked if we could meet then, last night instead of tonight, and I thought, Oh, what the hell, I might as well get this over with.

So I met him at a bar near where I live. I wore a black T-shirt, old patched jeans, and clogs. I think I sensed from the brief discussion we'd had over the phone that I would not be, to coin creepy Joel's phrase, "dressing like he liked." Even though I thought I looked good, I probably did it just to alienate him. I looked like a complete hippie.

Actually, I find the whole '60s look really attractive. I spent a good portion of my college career in long, flowing Indian skirts, a faded denim jacket, and Birkenstocks. I spent my 21st birthday at a Grateful Dead show. I still remember the set list.

Anyway, he looked like the pointy, little round-shouldered nerd he was, and I usually like the nerdy look but only if there's something sexy and intellectual or authoritative about the guy. I hate that weasley thing he had. And as I think about it, I realize now, looking back, that he seemed pretty psyched about how I looked, and it was only once I began speaking that he was totally turned off. It was so bad, and there was so little chemistry or stuff to talk about, that at some point I asked him, "So would you say this is the worst date you've had, or just close?"

The stupid gnome just smiled patronizingly. And then, because he's a doctor, and since there was nothing better to discuss, I found myself talking a lot about medicine and fellowships and hospitals—all stuff I know about from

David. And consequently, I also found myself speaking at length about David. And realizing that, I said, "It probably sounds like I am still hung up on my old boyfriend." And again, he smiled patronizingly, and I added, "I think it's because I am." And I was joking but he was making me so uncomfortable. It's not his fault that he's dull, or that he's not into me, or that there is no chemistry, but somehow it made me angry. Maybe I was disappointed, or felt rejected like *You should like me even though I've been nothing but sarcastic, boring, and bitter since I walked in.*

So we had one drink, and I tried to pay for mine but, happily, he wouldn't let me, and I thanked him and we shook hands goodnight. I think part of what was wrong was that it was just such a waste of time. I could've been home writing, or sleeping, or watching TV. And I was going to say that it was necessary for me to get together with him to ascertain that it was a waste of time, like maybe it could've been really good and then I'd be happy; but, honestly, I knew over the phone that there was no connection. So I don't know why I went. I guess it was just something to do. That, or hope springs eternal.

WHEN I GOT HOME FROM WORK TODAY, there was a message on the answering machine from Ben. It just said, *Hi, it's Ben. I'll drop off your stuff later today or tomorrow. Bye.* He sounded kind of pissed or inconvenienced. But fuck him. They are my things, and I don't think I should have to forfeit them just because he doesn't want to go out with me anymore. I really think it will give me some closure. If I have my things and no reason to call, I can just try to forget about him. I don't like the idea of him having them. It's just weird, like we're not together anymore, so let's not share intimate shit, like my bras. And I think he'll probably drop them off tomorrow instead of tonight, which would be better because hopefully he'll do it when I'm out, since tonight I am home for the evening. And I know that, when he drops them off, he won't make any attempt to see me. But I've locked the door and purposely remained untidy and undressed, so that if he did want to see me, my slovenly appearance and my vanity would shield me from temptation. Because I don't think I should see him.

I know I should just get over him, but I still can't believe how abruptly it all ended. Our relationship had been so intense. Maybe that's why it ended. But he loved me so much. . .for that week or so. And sometimes I think one cannot truly love a person in such a short period of time. But then I think, there is no rule about what is the proper amount of time two people must spend together before they can officially deem themselves "in love." Human emotion is a free-for-all, and it all depends on the people. Two weeks can be as good as two months or two years, depending on who is involved.

What's the point of wondering whether or not it was love, anyway? I mean, true love or not, it's over. I don't know whether I want to think it wasn't love so I have an easier time moving on, or if I'd rather think it *was* love so that I can wallow more. Both have their appeal.

And, yes, I know which is the healthy approach. Better not to wallow. And better still, not to *want* to wallow—although, in a way, it is harder to move on if I don't think it was love even more than if I do, but I'm not sure why. Like, before, I thought, If I tell myself it wasn't love but just a good time, or infatuation, I'll get over it more easily. But now I think maybe the way to get over it is by thinking it *was* love. I can't explain it, and anyway I am rapidly returning to my original theory—that it's easier to deal with if I chalk it up as something superficial. In fact, I've now almost completely changed my mind about the I-will-heal-more-easily-if-I-think-it-was-love approach. That can't be the way it works. It did make some vague sense for a while though.

And while I am on the subject of what is and isn't healthy, I ate well today. Still probably less than I should have, but there's been a marked improvement. In the morning, I had a small Greek salad. I didn't eat all the feta cheese or olives, but I had some, so I wasn't eating only lettuce and tomatoes. There were no anchovies, luckily, since I love them (or do I just think I love them?). And I ate both the stuffed grape leaves, and I know I love those babies. Then for lunch, I went to the gourmet deli near the office and bought a quarter pound of tuna with broccoli and a quarter pound of grilled veggies. And I'm sure the tuna dish had a lot of fat from the mayonnaise, and the vegetables were soaking in no small amount of oil, but I still think it was pretty healthy. I'm not eating anything else today, though. And I've lost about three or four pounds since I've begun writing, actually less than I expected to. Also, whenever I have the time or energy, I walk to wherever I have to go, provided it's not too far. And when it is too far, I try to make myself walk at least part of the way.

Recently, actually yesterday, I bought a book called *A Writer's Guide to Book Publishing* by a guy named Richard Balkin. It's all about how to get published and, even though I find it really informative and interesting, it's left me a bit pessimistic about the prospect of anyone besides family and friends ever reading this. And the friends-able-to-read-this circle is forever narrowing because I keep writing bad things about them. So eventually, I'll be a little lonely (but svelte) old lady with an increased number of cats and maybe, by then, a laptop, writing about the day that boy—that delightful young man. . .what was his name? Oh, yes! Sven—left me.

But then, too, I wonder, Could I get this published? Would it be of interest to anyone? It might be boring. Sometimes even *I* find it a bit dull, and that must be a bad sign. It sure as hell ain't a how-to book. Or at least it's no How-To-Anything-Anyone-Would-Want-To book. Like,

How-To-Develop-and-Sustain-an-Eating-Disorder, or How-To-Be-So-Self-Absorbed-You-Can-Barely-Function, or How-To-Smoke-All-the-Cigarettes.

And what is my motive for wanting it published? While talking to John a few days ago, I said, "It would be great if I could make money writing, because I love to write, and if someone paid me to do it, then I would have what everybody wants—a job they love." I guess it's not a bad thing to want. But I shouldn't concentrate too heavily, really not at all, on the publishing thing, because it will definitely affect what and how I write, and *that* I totally don't want because the therapeutic value of this is still my main concern.

But is it? In that book on publishing, I came across a part about editors sometimes wanting changes made before they agree to publish something. And I thought, That wouldn't be a problem for me. I would change some stuff, like *everything*, in order to get published. But I've got to get out of that mindset because, at least for the time being, I'm writing for me and no one else. And now I'm on the phone with John and I don't have anymore to write.

Goodnight.

# MORNING #18

ATE MORE LAST NIGHT after I stopped writing. I was really hungry, and there was practically no food in the house. So I took a fat-free Nabisco Raspberry Newton and wrapped some fat-free cheese around it—and it was so good! I had like three or four of those creations.

And this morning I had a stomach ache, and I thought, "Well, of course, serves me right since I binged last night." But it was hardly a binge, and it's probably harmful to even refer to it as such. Needless to say, I still—not intellectually, you know, but emotionally—feel I displayed a complete lack of will power, for which I will have to overcompensate today. This is *Morning Crazy Talk* with your self-loathing host. . . Jessica Kozner!

On the phone with John last night, I felt really sorry for him because I can relate to him, but I'm not in love with him. I told him about my date from the personal ad. Often, I find that I do things like that, mean-seeming things, with the intention of sparing another person's feelings, or to be honest to let them know me and what I'm actually about. I knew it was sort of mean to tell John I'd had a date, but I thought it was meaner to let him think I don't see anyone beside him, or that I'm not looking.

Anyway, he took it badly and asked, "Why are you dating other people? Don't you have a great time with me? Don't you think I'm special?"

And I do have so much fun with him, and I do think he's unique and special (and maybe gay). But for some reason, it's just not there. I'm sure the fact that he totally begs for my affection is no help. I said, "Look, if we decide to see only each other, there has to be a discussion first in which we agree that that's what we want to do. It's not like you and I are seeing each other, and I stop seeing you to go out with Ben, Ben and I break up, and then you and I are, like, automatically a couple. We have to spend time together and hang out. It has to evolve. You know, we've never spent a whole day together. I mean, I know you're busy with law stuff, but I don't think a bunch of late evenings out, or in, sipping coffee, is enough to base a relationship on."

"But I feel like we've spent enough time together to know that I want to be with you."

I knew what he meant. And he's right. He'd found the

flaw in my argument, which was a pretty mediocre one to begin with. His point was that he doesn't need to do everything with me to know that he'd like to do everything with me. He doesn't have to spend an entire afternoon with me to know how he feels about spending an entire afternoon with me.

Naturally, if I thought I loved him, I'd be ecstatic, and we'd be in perfect agreement. But I don't love him in that way, though the more I go out and see how bleak it is for single women, or at least for me, the more I think maybe I should *try* to love him like that.

So I'm sort of stalling for time. Time either to love him or to meet someone else before he tires of this game. I know that sounds really pathetic. But he is such a sweet and caring guy. And I do think he's very bright. And he does make me laugh. And he's my age, not practically a child, like Ben. And he's a lawyer. I mean, pathetic or not, it would be great if I could love him.

As I sit here, I realize I haven't really mentioned my father. Actually, he's my stepfather, but he and Mom married when I was about one or two years old, so he is the closest thing I have to a dad. In fact, he is Dad. I call him "Dad."

Something I pride myself on, in fact, is that even at fourteen or fifteen, when I was at my most obnoxious and bitchy, when he and I would clash, it never occurred to me to say, "You're not my father." He just was. Even if I thought he was being a stupid, stubborn asshole, I would tell him so, but I never told him he wasn't my dad. And I wasn't trying to spare his feelings, believe me. It just never crossed my mind. I'm sure it would've hurt him a great deal, so I am glad I never thought to say it, because, knowing me, I definitely would have. Actually, as I read this, I realize that there's nothing to pride myself on if I simply didn't think to say it. It's not like I was holding back, showing kindness or restraint.

Anyway, it just never happened. Or if I did, I blocked it out, because the thought of hurting this guy who has been nothing but loving, supportive, and generous my whole life is awful.

There isn't much to say about Dad. He's been wonderful to me. He has treated me, not as well as, but better than, the three kids he has from his first marriage. I know they don't think as highly of him as I do, and they did get the short end of the father-stick. But that isn't my problem. So it's not as if I don't think he has faults, it's just that I haven't been the recipient of any of his post-divorce venom or malice. He hates his ex-wife. And while I don't know her, I assume his perspective is somewhat skewed. Still, if any of what he says is to be believed, she does not sound like a prize, certainly not as a wife, and I know nothing about her as a mother.

Oh, dear. I just called Dad and read this little excerpt to him, and two horrible things happened. It went like this:

Dad: Honey, that's lovely. That really is sweet.

Me: And it's true too, isn't it? I never pulled the You're- Not-My-Father thing, did I?

Dad: Well, that's not important. What matters is, I'm so proud of you and Mommy. And I love you both so much."

Me: Yeah, that is so nice. But I never told you you're not my father, did I? Because I never thought it. (At this point I'm feeling the onset of guilt mingled with some skepticism.)

Dad: It doesn't matter. You were growing up. I didn't always take everything you and Mommy said seriously. I took it in context.

Me: Oh, fuck you. You ruined the whole thing. So, I said it?

Dad: (Laughing) You were a child, and you said certain things that, if I didn't consider you a child, would have been hurtful. But I always knew you loved me.

Me: Shit. That's great! So. . .what? Did I say it all the time? Was it, like, all I said for years? You're obviously still hurt by it.

Dad: (Still laughing) Listen, you've been a wonderful

daughter. You and Mommy have given me the best twenty-some-odd years of my life.

So that was awful. And what's worse is that I'm not entirely sure I believe him. I know it's possible that I've conveniently forgotten lots of mean things I've said to him over the years, but I think it is also possible that he just seized the opportunity to make me feel guilty. Maybe that sounds crazy, but I really think it could be the case— that he saw I was vulnerable, wanted to remember my childhood and my relationship with him a certain way, and he ran with it. Unless it did happen, in which case, he must still be hurt by it or he would have let it go and let me think what I want.

But then it got even worse, and kind of eerie, too. He said: "You know, I had a dream the other night and it was very vivid. I dreamt that I was dying, and you and Mommy were there. Kind of like the time you both visited me in the recovery room after my kidney stone operation. And you both were crying by my bedside, and I said, 'Don't cry. You both have made me the happiest man in the world.' And it's the truth. You both *have* given me the best years of my life. So don't worry about anything. Daddy will take care of everything."

Jesus, man. And that's not even the weird part. A few days ago I was on the phone with Mom, and I heard Dad coughing in the background. He was really hacking, and

I asked, sort of as a joke, but I was worried too, "What is he doing? Dying?" But it's not a great joke since he's like sixty-eight or sixty-nine years old, very overweight, and he smokes a pipe and cigars all day, so he really may *be* dying.

And mom said solemnly, "I worry about that." And then she said, "I had a dream last night," and it was the same fucking dream! Like what the hell am I supposed to do here? And I think there's a possibility that she had the dream, told him about it, and now he's acting like he had it too, just to freak me out, or to get attention, or to make me feel guilty or worried. It's crazy to think he would do something like this, but then, it's also crazy that he would actually have the exact same dream. Do I all of a sudden reconsider my skepticism about the supernatural?

And if they did both have the same dream, well, then he's dying, right? But maybe he's not dying right *away*. Maybe it's just a warning that he should take better care of himself. Or it's a vision of what will happen when he *does* die, but it hopefully won't be for a long time. And I don't think he has life insurance, so I think it's a sign that I should get going with the self-sufficiency thing. And what if he never lives to see the grandchildren that I don't seem even close to giving him? It's so sad.

Maybe only Mom had the dream, told him about it, and he just thinks he had it. I want to call him to ask him if it was definitely *his* dream; maybe I misheard him and he *did* say that it was Mom's. But I know that's not what happened. Did they both have it? What does it mean if they did? Did I also have it but don't remember it?

And then, too, I have to live with the newfound knowledge that I used to tell this poor, dying guy, "You're not my father." Why did he have to tell me that? It's not nice. He knew how happy I was about never having said that. Fucking bubble-bursting, memory-wrecking, grateful-to-have-me-in-his-life, dying old man. I can't deal with this. It is such a drag. I've got to go to work so that I have enough money to pay for the funeral. And maybe from now on I'll try harder to love John. But maybe I'll wait to see if he passes the bar first. Shit.

I'M HOME FROM WORK. I am less weirded out by the dying-Dad thing. I don't know why. Maybe it's just that some time has passed. It does upset me, the prospect of Mom and Dad having the same dream about Dad dying. Then, too, the prospect of one, or both, of them lying about it is also unsettling. I didn't discuss with anyone because it gives me the creeps and I'd rather not think about it. I don't mind writing about it, though. That's one of the great functions of writing: You can write things to yourself that you wouldn't speak to other people.

Damn, I had a huge fight with this guy from my office just now over the phone. I totally yelled at him. Here's what happened: A couple of days ago, Luke, a pretentious, self-important twenty-year-old ass (who's been on the biggest ego trip since our boss Sam—whom I fucked a couple of times but no one in the office knows, especially since he's engaged—made him manager), asked me, "What ever happened to Ben?"

I sighed, "Yeah, he doesn't call here anymore because we broke up. I'd rather not discuss it."

Luke is one of those people who clearly revels in other people's misfortune so he is the last person I want to confide in.

Anyway, today, Abigail called the office looking for me, and Luke answered the phone. "Well," he merrily told her, "she doesn't have a beeper in service anymore or I'd page her for you. But I can tell you that she's not with Ben."

I know this because I just spoke with Abigail. When she told me, I was furious. Yes, she already knew that Ben and I had broken up, but what if she hadn't? Who else is he telling? And what right does he have to gossip about me, anyway?

I immediately got off the phone with her to call the office. Richard, another agent, answered. I asked for Luke, and Richard said he was with a client. So I asked to speak with Sam, because I was going to complain about Luke, but Luke picked up the phone first. And totally unaware of my mood and his wrongdoing, he was all, "Hi Sweetie. Your friend Abigail called—"

"I know. That's why I'm calling." And I hauled off and

started totally yelling at him. I practically shouted, "What the hell business is it of yours whether or not I'm with Ben or where I am when I'm out of the office? It so happens that Abigail knows about the break-up, but it's just so un-professional and inappropriate for you to be telling people about my personal life! I mean, I know I'm not perfect, and I can be irresponsible, and I don't always show up when I say I will, but you never hear me telling people about *your* fucking private life, do you? I've really had it. It's like working with a fucking six-year-old. This shit is none of your business in the *first* place and it's even *less* your place to *share with the world!*" And I hung up on him. It felt really good.

At some point in that conversation he'd quietly said, "I'm sorry." But fuck that. I was furious. Now I'm on the phone with John, and I have to go.

I'M BACK. I JUST SPOKE TO MOM. It was both a relief and also a bit anti-climactic. Turns out *she* never had the dream. Only *Dad* had it. It's good to know they didn't both dream that Dad's dying. I guess she was telling me about his dream and I just misheard and mistook it for hers.

I'm kind of drunk right now. For lunch, I had a pre-pared Fairway salad with a couple of slices of roast beef, and then I bought a bottle of cheap white wine on my way home and drank all of it. I also had a glass of wine with Amy after work at the All State. There are probably a lot of calories in wine, but I didn't have a big lunch. And that's all I ate today. That's not too healthy, and I was drunk when I just spoke to Mom, and she could tell. But I wasn't embarrassed because I've talked to her when she was loaded with pills and slurring her words, too. And it was really good to talk to her anyway because now I know they didn't both have that same death dream.

Ben didn't drop off my clothes today as he said he would, and that really annoys me. Why can't he just keep his word and get out of my life? Why did he say he'd drop them off? The most painful part is that it was probably just not convenient for him, so he didn't bother. But I *am* the one who's reluctant to believe anything is just an accident, or coincidence, or luck, so maybe there's more to it than that.

I guess I don't want to get my hopes up. I'd like to think that Ben somehow hangs onto my clothes and stuff for a symbolic reason, but I'm sure that's not the case. And who cares by now? It's so moot. In fact, today, I was contemplating whether or not I'd even take him back if he asked me. And I thought, No, that would not be in my best interest. But I still wish he would just love me again, because it was so much fun. Will I have that kind of fun again?

I assume anyone reading this will think, Of *course* you will, silly.

But it's not easy to feel confident when you're living it.

# EVENING #19

'M BACK FROM WORK. I actually have been back for a while. Amy just left. As I mentioned, she's a Buddhist. We did evening Gongyo together. It's just reciting the prayers and chanting *Nam Myoho Renge Kyo* a lot. We've done it before. I like the way it sounds, but it's hard for me to follow along because she reads so fast and I'm not familiar with the pronunciation. But she always says, "Just do the best you can, and don't worry about how you sound, because it's just me here. And anyway, you'll receive benefits from making even the slightest effort."

I like the idea of it, but I'm not sure I buy it. For me, the appeal is the rhythm of the chanting. It's so relaxing and soothing. Hearing the prayers puts me in kind of a trance. I also like that you can pray for anything you want. As far as my understanding goes, it's the effort of chanting that's rewarded. So it's the chanting that counts. It doesn't matter if you're chanting for money, for fame, or for Ben to come crawling back. I like that about it.

It was a little awkward in the office today since my outburst with Luke last night. We didn't speak to each other when I came in, but when I left to show the studio—that albatross I can't seem to rent—I said "goodbye" to him, just to be the bigger person. And he said it back. That idiot. And I think I'm as pissed as I am (although I'm really not anymore) because he's done things like this in the past.

And the answer is not, "So don't share things with him," because I didn't. He asked me about Ben. What was I supposed to do? I could've said, "It's none of your business," but that's rude and also it's basically telling him that Ben and I broke up. I could've said, "Ben's fine," but there would've been more questions like, "How come he never calls here anymore?" And *then* I could've said, "It's none of your business," but the problem with saying it then remains the same. So I don't know how to completely exclude a meddling co-worker. Of course, I doubt he'll be too troublesome now that he either hates me or thinks I'm nuts, or both. It's a relief.

Lately, I've noticed that I'm especially bitter and intolerant of others. It's always been the case, but even more so recently. I mean, I do think that the people I badmouth are objectionable and have done genuinely objectionable things, but I don't like that I am so quick to anger. And why am I even wasting all this emotion on them if I think they're so inferior or inconsequential?

Like, I do think Liz should've taken Olga's adultery story less seriously. And Luke shouldn't be chatting at the office about my break-up. And Abigail is somewhat spacey. But I don't think I should mind as much as I do. I'm sure it has to do with some bullshit, which is completely true, about my not being happy with myself.

On the other hand, I think it's good that I express myself to people who I feel have wronged me, like Luke for example. In the past, I wouldn't have said anything. I'd have just seethed and complained to everyone else. This way, at least, I get it off my chest right away. And I say it directly to the offender. Maybe my flying off the handle with Luke signifies the beginning of my taking charge of my life, and it's just that I need some practice conveying my feelings more calmly and appropriately. Luke may have been a guinea pig. I tested the self-expression waters on him. But I don't want to be this really hateful person who can't even weather the slightest conflict or discomfort.

I have no idea what I just wrote because I put the stereo on in the other room and I can't concentrate at all when there's music playing, even softly. I put the stereo on knowing I wouldn't know what I was writing, but I felt lonely and thought it would keep me company.

The TV is better for that. Usually, I put the TV on in

the other room and mute it. And then I can write with the knowledge that there's something going on elsewhere in the apartment. It's comforting. I just like knowing that it's there, that warm, flickering TV glow. And occasionally I take a break and stroll in to look briefly at what's going on, but it really doesn't matter since I just like that it's showing *something*. Is this what I do in relationships? Pay too little attention to what they're "showing" and put too much emphasis on whether they're just there and "on"? I don't have the energy to explore this right now. It's more unpalatable food for thought. Or not.

Speaking of food, today I had a Fairway spinach salad that was very nice, and lots of liquids like water, soda, juice, and iced coffee, since it's so damn hot out. I feel fat. I feel full. I also had the last piece of fat-free cheese wrapped around a fat-free Newton. These are so tasty, even though they're also a bit gross. Kim just got here, so I have to go.

I'M BACK! KIM CAME OVER with her sister, Christine, and Christine's two friends, Paula and Bonnie. They had been out to dinner. It was a small bachelorette party for Christine, who's getting married in a little under a month. They came back to my place to get high and kill some time before going over to the Comic Strip. As per the plan, I went along. I was really nervous about going because I was afraid I might see Ben. I wanted to see him too. But I felt sick to my stomach at the thought of bumping into him, especially if he were with a woman (yes, I know I've said this before).

But the prospect of him being there, not even on a date but say, with some friends whom I've met and used to hang out with, also upset me. I used to be part of that group. They were my friends too, at least when we were together.

But Ben wasn't at the club, and I think it was better that way. I wondered at some point, What if he's here and he sees me and he's avoiding having me notice him? That would be so painful. But not really, if he did a good enough job of avoiding me, because then I wouldn't know.

And then Tammy, Kim's brother's girlfriend, showed up as the show was ending. And Tammy, Kim, and her sister Christine came back to my place. And first of all, Tammy is crazy and aggressive and annoying. But that doesn't matter. As I was sitting there with them, I realized that Kim is married, that Christine is getting married, and that even crazy Tammy has a boyfriend. And I don't have anyone. I was feeling sorry for myself. And I wonder if I'm totally romanticizing the whole Ben thing. Maybe I've blown it completely out of proportion. But it's so easy to do when you don't have someone else. On the one hand, the relationship was so short that it's hard to believe I'm taking this break-up so badly. But on the other, it having been as short as it was means I didn't have time to tire of him or start squabbling with him over nonsense.

When I think of it that way, it's easy to understand how I can still think about him so much. Since it never had a chance to get bad, as it very well might have, I have only good memories of fun and frolicking.

Still, I wish I had never met him. And to be perfectly honest, I think I'm both horrified and comforted by the fact that I feel his having come from money probably influenced my opinion of him. *Definitely* did, in fact. I'm horrified because I don't want to think that wealth would affect my feelings for another person. But then, how could it not? I mean, it's bad if it's *why* you like someone. But it's okay if you like them already and just view it as a bonus, isn't it? How could it not make even a slight difference? It must. But maybe I'm comforted by thinking money was a factor because then maybe I *didn't* really care for Ben, the person, as much as I think I did. So losing him is not as bad as all that.

But, unfortunately, I know that I liked him independent of the money. Other guys with money have liked me and I haven't necessarily liked them back. I mean, growing up, everyone had money. So it sucks, because I lost Ben and the money. And I'm comfortable with having liked them both. Shit.

I think that tomorrow I'm going to look for another job. Either I'll try to work at a different real estate agency, or I'll try to do something altogether different. I'm dissatisfied, and the turnover there has made it less and less fun, and more and more cutthroat and sleazy. I assume I'll find that in any real estate office, but maybe to a lesser degree, or maybe in a subtler form. The office used to feel like the cast from *Taxi*. It was such a weird mélange. There's Liz, the recent Columbia law grad who was taking a little time before she had to start her hundred-hour-a-week-until-she-retired-at-fifty job at Skadden or somewhere. Amy, the pot-smoking Jewish Buddhist with the abusive mom, eating disorder, and seemingly imaginary boyfriend. There's Luke, so annoying and pompous but still wonderfully gay and flamboyant and always armed with a biting remark or observation. There's Sam, the boss. He's boring, tightly wound, engaged to a girl just like him, and the most interesting thing about him, for me, is that I fucked him. I don't even mention Rick because he's so rarely in the office. He's scruffy and druggy, a cross between Bobby Wheeler and Jim Ignatowski.

Once when we were in the office with nothing to do, he offered me what I thought was coke and I snorted it. I immediately felt sweaty and lightheaded, so I rushed outside for air and promptly puked between two parked cars on West Eighty-sixth Street. I think he told me after that it was heroin. Anyway, that's Rick. There are so many stories, but they're not about Ben, so they'll have to wait. This business just seems to attract a lot of misfits and braggarts and liars. And I feel out of place, since I think I only belong in the first category, if any.

When we were headed for the Comic Strip, I nudged Kim and asked her, "If we see Ben with a woman, will you please grab my hand?" My joke was that I didn't want to seem like I didn't also have a date. And we laughed as my stomach churned with anxiety. I added, "Actually, if we see Ben, would you ask him to return my stuff?" And we laughed some more.

Once we were at our table, having already scanned the place and not seen him, I couldn't stop watching the door to see if he was coming in. As she watched me watch the door, I noted, "He's so short, I wouldn't be able to spot him anyway." But, short or not, I think he's wonderful looking. He may not be the best-looking guy I've ever seen, but there is something so beautiful about his features and the way he carries himself. He walks much older than he is. Money.

Why do I care so much? I don't think it's anything as simple as, "You loved him." There's something else going on. Of course, that something else may be that I'm bored. There's no other game in town at the moment. I mean, we really did have a good time. I know I'm not making that up. But he's not the only guy I've ever had fun with. I mean, I'm acting like he's my first boyfriend or someone much more memorable than a kid I dated for a few lively months. Why does it have to be such a big deal? I guess because I'm *making* a big deal of it. But why am I doing that? Do I just want to pine away for someone? Or did I really love him, and this is a normal reaction?

I'm really sleepy and going to bed soon, but it totally sucks that the more I think about our time together, the more I feel like there were signs that Ben was pulling away and I just chose to ignore them. As I go over it, I realize that the change in his behavior was not as abrupt as I first took it to be. Granted, when a relationship only spans a couple of months, everything is abrupt. Going out is abrupt. Breaking up is abrupt. There was nothing long and drawn-out about our affair. But I think it's good that I realize this. And I think it's especially good because I am not using this newfound awareness to chastise myself, like: "You see, you had warning. You could've fixed it had you paid closer attention." No, instead I feel it's a good thing to know because it makes me feel less responsible. Like: "Relax, it's no *one* thing you did. The guy was twenty-three. He couldn't commit because of him, not because of you."

Confession: Right after we broke up, I thought that he was turned off because of one particular day when I was really bitchy and harsh to him. He was at my place, and he was bugging me about something, some movie he wanted to rent or place he wanted to go. Or it might have been that he was rushing me to get ready because he's allergic to my cats. Whatever the cause, I blocked it out, but I remember saying something like, "Look, if you don't like it, you can leave. In fact, I think maybe you should go."

It was totally uncalled for, I remember that much. We were both shocked by my cold, detached tone. It was not in the least bit justified. Nothing he did or said warranted it. And in retrospect, I wasn't even upset with him, it was more like an experiment. I think it was either me trying to sabotage the relationship, or maybe in some fucked-up way, testing him—like how far can I go and have him stay? How dysfunctional can I be with this guy? If it was sabotage, I succeeded.

Was I testing his love or commitment? Some small part of me even wonders if I was just trying to be interesting or dramatic: "Ooh, I'm so complicated and fiery. Isn't it exciting? Love me."

Anyway, I thought that things were never quite the same after my brief possession or whatever it was. And perhaps they weren't. But I now realize there had been signs even before that, and maybe that was just the icing on the cake, the straw that broke the camel's back. Maybe he was already weirded out by having a girlfriend and he was looking to get out. Maybe this convinced him that he was right to want to split, or he was already sure and this just helped him do it with less guilt or uncertainty. Maybe he thought, She's crazy, so I should get out before we get even more serious.

I wonder if it isn't crazy to be thinking all these things in the first place. It doesn't matter, because I'm really glad I wrote this tonight. It was a painful and embarrassing admission, but I'm glad I confronted these feelings. I'm Stuart Smalley. I'm also going to bed.

# EVENING #20

'M HOME FROM A LONG DAY away from home. First, I
went to work. I think I may have finally rented the studio! Then I went to Kim's and hung out with her at her
place. And then Kim and I went down to hang out with
her in-laws. They are Steve's mom Helen and her husband
Michael. Steve also has a half-brother and a stepbrother.

It was fun. They have a huge open-space loft in Soho.
I think the building had been a factory of some sort.
Helen made dinner and we played charades. It was nice
to see them again, since I hadn't been down to their place
in a while.

They both do something high tech with computers,
multi-media imaging or something. But Kim was out with
them the other night and mentioned my story to them.
Michael expressed an interest in it, asked to read it, and
said maybe he could do something with it. He has an idea

to put it on the computer and people can read the whole thing or maybe just access specific parts of it under different headings like *Emotions*.

So there would be a *Sorrow* category and a *Jealousy* one and a *Happiness* one and so on. And then there would be pictures or images to accompany the text.

So that would be kind of like being published. Actually, I guess it *would* be being published. This could be very exciting. But I worry about losing control of this "project." When we discussed it, it seemed like my involvement in the whole thing would be very limited. Once we agreed to how much money I would get, my work was essentially done. At that point I'd turn it over to all the other people who would take it from there. And I don't know if that's actually what *would* happen. I also don't know if it's so bad if that's how it *does* happen. I have no idea how the whole publishing thing works. Maybe this would be the same deal anywhere. And if this handling of my work is unique, that isn't necessarily a bad thing. As Mom would say, it should be the biggest problem I ever have.

But I do feel somewhat reluctant to write at length about being published because I don't want to get my hopes up. Also, getting published is not what this is about.

Well, it *wasn't*; maybe now it is. At first I thought, I don't want to spend a lot of time writing about getting published because that's getting away from the point, which is to help me cope with all the different feelings I have right now about my life, and the break-up, and my general dissatisfaction.

But then, I write about what's going on, and if the possibility of this new venture is what's going on, I want to be able to write about it, too. But I fear hoping to be published may change the way I write. I worry that I'll start writing as if for an audience and not just for me. But maybe that's okay, too.

Some more unsettling thoughts: If Kim's husband and in-laws are helping me to do something with my writing, I can't really write bad things about them, can I? Not that I have anything bad to say right now, but in fairness, I would be surprised if nary a negative thought did cross my mind. And they'll be privy to every word of it. There is nothing from which I could exclude them if we turn this into a joint project.

Not only that, I already feel—and would even moreso if anything lucrative came of this—somewhat indebted to them for even being willing to help me. Maybe I shouldn't feel indebted; I mean, if any good came of it, my writing would benefit them, too. But I feel it anyway. And that, in addition to the fact that they're Kim's family, makes it even harder to write without censoring myself. But then, if I were pursuing having this published under ordinary circumstances, I would feel the same reluctance to write about the publishers or editors with whom I came in contact. If I got an agent, I'm sure I wouldn't feel comfortable writing about difficulties with her knowing that she's going to read it. So maybe it's just something I have to work out on my own, having nothing to do with who's involved.

The plan is for Kim to edit. And I worry that she and I will have all sorts of style conflicts, and that too many, or just one bad one, could really strain our friendship, like end it.

And then I wonder, Is it worth it to lose Kim to gain some money or notoriety? And the answer, I suppose, unless it's a whole lot of money, is "no." But that would be irrelevant, because if Kim and I had a huge fight, wouldn't her husband and father-in-law stop working with me anyway? So I guess I couldn't lose her friendship and still get the money or recognition.

Maybe if we had something good going we'd keep working together and just be icy and professional, like those rock bands that keep touring even after they all hate each other. But that would suck—working with people I've hurt or alienated.

And I have to admit now, it did kind of weird me out that, while discussing this project, it seemed like my role was far smaller and less important than everyone else's. But I guess it would be that way anywhere since all I can do is write and I know nothing about computers or editing or publishing. I guess in terms of a project, what I'm doing right now, writing, is my input, my job. And then, as is appropriate, everyone else does theirs.

Now I feel embarrassed about having written what I just wrote. Not because I think these feelings are shameful or unnatural, but because probably nothing will come of this proposal, and I have just spent a lot of time worrying about nonsense. And now, whether they do or don't use this, they'll definitely read it, because that has to happen before they decide if and where they want to go with it. And I've just written about what a drag it is that I can't say shit about them, and that I want to be able to make all the decisions regarding stuff about which I know nothing.

I feel strangely humbled but still a bit constricted as well. The one good thing: I'm confident that these feelings are not specifically related to Michael, or Steve, or Kim, or Helen. Like, if some random, unrelated, person took an interest in doing something with my story, I would immediately feel a loss of liberty regarding what I could write about him or her as well. So it doesn't have anything to do with these individuals.

And I don't know why I can't ever just look on the bright side: "Gee, I get to participate in something really neat with people I really like." As excited as I am, I've focused almost solely upon my concerns. I mean, this could be a wonderful thing for us all, in terms of our friendship, as well as career stuff or money. Working together can enhance a friendship. Can't it? But already, all I see is my friendship with Kim ending and all of them never speaking to me again. This seems silly, but there is a real danger in working with friends, isn't there? Maybe, like everything else, it's what you make it.

This is getting really boring.